BALDWIN'S HARLEM

BALDWIN'S HARLEM

A BIOGRAPHY
OF JAMES BALDWIN

HERB BOYD

ATRIA BOOKS
NEW YORK LONDON TORONTO SYDNEY

ATRIA BOOKS

A Division of Simon & Schuster, Inc.
1230 Avenue of the Americas
New York, NY 10020

First Atria Books trade paperback edition January 2009

ATRIA BOOKS and colophon are trademarks
of Simon & Schuster, Inc.

For credits and permissions, please see page 234.

For information about special discounts for bulk purchases,
please contact Simon & Schuster Special Sales at
1-800-456-6798 or business@simonandschuster.com.

Designed by C. Linda Dingler

Manufactured in the United States of America

10 9 8 7 6 5 4 3 2 1

ISBN-13: 978-0-7432-9307-5
ISBN-13: 978-0-7432-9308-2 (pbk)

To: ELZA, THE KATHERINES, AND THE BALDWINS

CONTENTS

FOREWORD

By Peniel E. Joseph

Perhaps more than any other writer before or since, James Baldwin distilled the anger, pain, and passion of black life in America and beyond. As an essayist, playwright, and novelist Baldwin forever transformed public commentary and political inquiry on issues of race, violence, and democracy.

As a public intellectual Baldwin dialogued with Malcolm X, marched with Martin Luther King, Jr., defended black student demonstrators, and predicted that the United States would hasten its own demise if it failed to practice democracy within its own borders. During the civil rights movement's heroic years, Baldwin rose to become the official transcriber of a blues people engaged in daily combats against personal insults, political indignities, and physical violence.

Baldwin's success also announced the arrival of a literary

maverick and intellectual provocateur bold enough to consort with the likes of Malcolm X, Elijah Muhammad, and Martin Luther King, Jr. His growing literary notoriety, acceptance by the mainstream intellectual establishment, and personal friendships with leading black political activists made him a target of some critics who accused him of exaggerating black misery to a largely white audience. Such critics confused Baldwin's fierce compassion with surrender; mistook vivid, grim descriptions of Harlem as stereotyping; and regarded the writer's celebrity as undeserved. By the early 1960s, diverse groups of writers and intellectuals, from black nationalists in Ghana to white liberals in New York City, debated the power and passion of Baldwin's writing and his growing significance as a public intellectual.

"Time catches up with kingdoms and crushes them," warned Baldwin in his best-known work, *The Fire Next Time*. Published in 1963 and hailed as a masterpiece of social criticism, Baldwin's book challenged America to turn words into deeds and, failing that, excoriated the national hypocrisy that fostered white guilt without corresponding justice, and black death without corresponding remorse. Baldwin's timing proved prophetic. The year 1963 was one of turbulence punctuated by racial violence in Birmingham, Alabama, the assassination of civil rights leader Medgar Evers, the murder of four little black girls at Birmingham's Sixteenth Street Baptist Church, and the November 22 assassination of John F. Kennedy.

But Baldwin's words of fire also held out hope for racial reconciliation. If Malcolm X served as black America's prosecuting attorney, collectively indicting whites for past crimes that could be traced back to antebellum slavery, Baldwin passionately pled for a stay of execution. *The Fire Next Time* established Baldwin as the preeminent black writer of his generation and tied him to the civil rights insurgency rapidly transforming America's domestic priorities and national character. In May 1963, Attorney General Robert F. Kennedy tapped Baldwin to organize a doomed attempt at racial diplomacy.

In an effort to gauge the pulse of black folk, Kennedy asked Baldwin to organize a meeting with leading cultural and literary figures that included Lorraine Hansberry, Harry Belafonte, Lena Horne, and Professor Kenneth B. Clark. The meeting disintegrated into a raucous shouting match with many in the room criticizing the Kennedy administration's tentative civil rights policies. Baldwin's role as Kennedy's personal, if also uncontrollable, emissary raised Baldwin's stature at the expense of the attorney general, whom one critic chided as "the little man who wasn't there."

Widely recognized as an ardent supporter of civil rights, Baldwin was equally committed to black radicalism. After Baldwin's speech at the March on Washington was censored, Malcolm X paid him the ultimate compliment, remarking that Baldwin was prevented from speaking at the event because "he was liable to say anything."

And such was often the case. Whether arguing that the sit-in movement raging across the South in the early 1960s went beyond "the consumption of overcooked hamburgers and tasteless coffee at various sleazy lunch counters," or defending the political right of Stokely Carmichael to protest against American racism, Baldwin remained an oracle of bold truths and uncomfortable insights. Like the prophet Jeremiah, Baldwin's Old Testament–style candor at times fell on deaf ears but was rarely dismissed. While many contemporaries rejected the bruising polemics of Black Power activists during the late 1960s, Baldwin embraced embattled young activists, including Carmichael and Angela Davis, as a new generation of radical visionaries.

Baldwin first encountered the racial demons he would publicly wrestle with on a national stage as a child in Harlem. Baldwin came of age in a Harlem that was past the prime of its New Negro heyday in which Garveyites, literary prodigies, and working-class black folk had forged new arenas of cultural achievement and social and political struggle. Poverty, restlessness, and unpredictable spasms of violence shadowed Baldwin's childhood. But Harlem also housed buried literary treasures, sidewalk street speakers extolling the virtues and values of a liberated future, and the hard-won courage etched in the faces of black men and women who remained defiant in the face of despair. Competing forces of hope and despair engaged in open combat on Harlem street corners. If despair claimed untold and undocumented lives during Baldwin's youth, hope saved the unusual-looking child with no memories of his biological father.

Harlem remains central to understanding James Baldwin's literary and political stature, impact, and resonance. Both Harlem's and James Baldwin's impact can be seen in the prodigious works of Detroit native and longtime Harlemite Herb Boyd. No writer is better able to begin the long-overdue task of connecting James Baldwin to his birthplace, and *Baldwin's Harlem* takes us to the corner of the world that indelibly shaped Baldwin's literary work and political activism. Boyd has navigated a complex, difficult undertaking with eloquence, verve, and style, transporting us back to an era that becomes increasingly blurred with the passage of time. For Boyd, Harlem and Baldwin remain forever linked through personal experience and literary imagination. Both the iconic neighborhood and iconic writer were permanently etched in the imagination, consciousness, and history of the other. At a moment when Harlem is undergoing a painful, at times invigorating, process of transformation whose end result remains unclear, remembering *Baldwin's Harlem* provides us an important window onto a past that may still provide, like Baldwin's writing, hopeful signposts into the future.

Preface

During this long travail
our ancestors spoke to us, and we listened,
and tried to make you hear life in our song
but now it matters not at all to me
whether you know what I am talking about—or not:
I know why we are not blinded
by your brightness, are able to see you
who cannot see us. I know
why we are still here.

–from "Staggerlee Wonders," *Jimmy's Blues*, James Baldwin

When I was a young man, one way in which James Baldwin almost immediately captured my attention was the image I had of him, that is, seeing him as a teenager with a book in one hand and a diaper in the other. While the book in his hand could have been something by Charles Dickens, Henry James, Mark Twain, Frederick Douglass, Richard Wright, Louisa May Alcott, or Harriet Beecher Stowe, the book in my hand was *Go Tell It on the Mountain, Notes of a Native Son,* or *Nobody Knows My Name.* I could relate to the incessant drama that filled many days of Baldwin's youth, minding his younger brothers and sisters, having them compete with Balzac, Faulkner, Chester Himes, and Ann Petry for his attention.

Another compelling aspect was his intense gaze, which often adorned the covers of his books. Even before I had leafed through the pages, it was his penetrating stare that commanded my attention, a stare from a face many had defined as less than attractive. But to me he was never ugly. If he were odd-looking, then so was I since in many respects we shared common features, though his were a bit more pronounced than mine with his eyes bulging like lamps from a prominent forehead that soared upwardly, shaped like a bullet, all of which was accentuated by a widow's peak. From his father's often demented perspective, though, all his stepson needed was a cloven hoof to complete his image of the devil. To some degree my own reflection in the mirror prepared me for Baldwin's imposing stare. His look matched his genius; he radiated a kind of inscrutable intelligence, like a brother from another planet. I accepted the fact that to possess such a profound vision he needed those eyes, and for him to have a different way of comprehending and then articulating our condition he had to look as though he had actually experienced all the terror and hurt a face could possibly bear. I knew he was the target of all the cruel abuse that innocent children can heap on their playmates. Dark, small, funny-looking, and timid, there was no sting of rejection he wasn't aware of or had not endured. He had my sympathy before I fell under the power of his words.

And his blizzard of words hit me with such force that I was often left dizzy, sometimes struggling to understand exactly what he meant. I was intoxicated by his lyrical, dazzling prose. His sentences were convoluted, layered, and so filled with mind-boggling sprints of language that even when I wasn't fully aware of what he was saying, it sounded so good, so astonishingly fresh that I would copy some of the sentences in my notebook, hoping some of his magic would rub off on me.

Baldwin altered so many things in my early years as I grappled with identity, purpose, and whether I had enough of what it took to be a man. Without a father or father figure, that reality for me changed daily. Coming of age in Detroit, my ideal of a great metropolis had been forged though my absorption of movies about Manhattan, particularly those ten-or fifteen-minute soundies featuring Louis Jordan, Nat King Cole, Count Basie, Duke Ellington, or Dizzy Gillespie. Bodies flying across the floors of large ballrooms, jitterbugging and Lindy-hopping to the break of day, or the big bands from the stage of the Apollo were my introductions to Harlem.

Then there was the search for books about Harlem that were not easy to find; even at the public library you were lucky to track down a book by a black writer. The first black writer I saw in the flesh, I think—and it may not have been him—was Clarence Cooper, who I was told lived on Wabash or a street nearby on Detroit's Westside. One day I stood outside the house waiting for him so I could see what a writer looked like. That day came sooner than I expected and I followed this hulking figure down the street; I was too terrified to say anything to him. He didn't look to be any older than I was, maybe in his early twenties, but no less foreboding in his carriage. Even from that distance there was something menacing about him, daring anyone to speak to him. Later, I scrounged up two of his books, *Weed* and *Black*. He would be a forerunner of a genre popularized by another writer I bumped into once in a pool hall, the late Donald Goines.

These literary overtures happened not too long after my high school days, when baseball was my other passion and I had nothing on my mind but how I would replace Harvey Kuenn as the shortstop for the Detroit Tigers. Ever since I was old enough to cross busy Joseph Campau Street and head into the heart of Hamtramck, a bastion of Polish Americans, it was to watch the Detroit Stars of the Negro Leagues; this was an opportunity to see black players, since there were none on the Tigers in those days. A man who worked in a cleaners on the North End—one of the several places where we lived that once more gave Baldwin and his ever-moving family a special place in my life—would come by our house from time to time to see my mother, and he played on the Stars. I loved the way he wore his stingy brim hat and cocked the baseball cap on his head. He didn't always play but he looked good in his uniform.

My next literary epiphany after devouring all of Baldwin and the writers of the Harlem Renaissance occurred when I was sixteen. One day I picked up a paper, the *Michigan Chronicle*, the city's black weekly, and saw a picture of Ron Milner. He was being touted as the next Langston Hughes or

James Baldwin. What made it all so improbable was that Ron and I had challenged each other in sports; our baseball rivalry was especially intense since he was the captain of an Eastside squad and I was the captain of the Westside recreational team that had won our division title. We had met in the championship game that year and my team won; our team had the choice of taking two of their players as we entered the regional finals. I liked Ron's fire and determination, but the manager wanted a catcher and an outfielder, where he felt we were weakest. To no avail, Dave DeBusschere, who would go on to play for the Chicago White Sox and the New York Knicks, had a fastball that I'm still, along with my teammates, waiting to see. We were soundly trounced, and I don't think Ron would have helped us much. But there he was in the paper. Not the fierce competitor on the baseball diamond but "an emerging writer," the paper announced. I thought I was alone in the love of books among my athletic friends or rivals. To talk about books back then in our macho crowd was to draw suspicious looks; such talk was akin to treason, or at least warranted a round of abuse and every foul name a fifteen-year-old mouth could muster.

Ron's exposure emboldened me. If he had the courage to admit he wanted to be a writer and wasn't afraid of being called a sissy, then maybe I could find the guts to do the same. In those days, Baldwin's homosexuality was not yet widely known, and I'm not sure how it would have affected me if I had known. When I later learned of his homosexuality, it didn't bother me since I had no real aversion to homosexuals and I was pretty secure in my own heterosexuality. Anything short of being a child molester or a murderer, Baldwin would have still appealed to me as a writer. It was not until Ron had gone on to become one of the nation's fore-most playwrights that the paths of our lives crossed. By now he had been blessed by Langston Hughes, had been to the Big Apple, and had discovered Harlem, while I was still dreaming and scheming how to get out of Detroit. Ron is gone now but his legacy has a permanent and enduring place in the pantheon of black theater, and in my treasury of memories.

Much of the glamour I gleaned of Harlem came from the writers associated with the Harlem Renaissance. They—Langston Hughes, George Schuyler, Zora Neale Hurston, Countee Cullen, and Claude McKay—had painted such a glorious tableau that even when I read Baldwin's often depressing accounts, my desire to see the community was not muted. Quite the contrary: some of Baldwin's denunciations even gave the enclave an added touch of danger. It was a haven, with the magnetism of a casbah. And besides, it couldn't be that bad; hadn't it produced Countee Cullen and Baldwin himself? So, Baldwin's negative descriptions only fueled a fire that burned incandescently for Harlem.

When I finally got to Harlem three years after graduating from high school and running from a deteriorating marriage, Baldwin was long gone. The Harlem he left behind was much worse than the one he had described. So, one of my dreams had been smacked down. Living in Brooklyn and the Village was much more appealing, and for a year and a half I enjoyed hanging with my boys in Bed-Stuy and the Beats in the Village, that is, until Uncle Sam broke up the party. Once more I was on the run from the draft, but it was futile; I surrendered, and rather than go to jail I chose the military.

With Baldwin's book in my back pocket, I took my oath

and spent most of the next twenty months of duty in Germany. If Baldwin could endure Paris, I could withstand the vagaries of Frankfurt, even the times when the German children surrounded me and called me the devil. I survived a dozen or so months of brutally cold weather, and as a "jock-strapper" (playing whatever sport was in season) I dodged a lot of KP and guard duty. I even beat a summary court-martial. After a trip to Tangier, trying to catch up with Malcolm X, who I was told would be arriving in Casablanca about the time I was there, I returned to Germany and was arrested for allegedly transporting drugs from Morocco to Germany. The evidence was incredible—I had several hashish pipes (used) that I brought back with me to give as gifts. I had planned to clean them, but the Army's Criminal Investigation Division ("El CID") beat me to it and the residue was Exhibit A. I wish I had the space here to relate exactly how I beat the charge, but it was mainly a mock trial conducted by my unit to get me out of the country so I would not have to be called as a witness and testify in the trials of some thirty other GIs who had been rounded up in a massive drug sweep across Germany.

Somehow, during these turbulent times, I got a French version of Baldwin's *Giovanni's Room,* and since I understood the language the delightful metaphors were enough to keep my mind occupied: it also kept Baldwin in my sight as I rode the highway of life back to Detroit and a few months at Dodge Main, a factory in Hamtramck. I was back in the briar patch.

My plan was to make enough money to move to Harlem, where Malcolm X was well along in establishing his Organization of Afro-American Unity and the Muslim Mosque, Inc.

I had met Malcolm on several occasions at the Temple Number One in Detroit, which he would visit after becoming a national minister for the Nation of Islam. When Malcolm left the Nation in 1964, I was among those who welcomed the move. Now he had his own organization and whether he was looking for recruits or not I was ready to sign. I knew too late of his plans to honor a speaking engagement in Detroit despite having had his house firebombed. During that stretch at the plant I was working a swing shift but mainly at night. Thus I was not able to attend Malcolm's speech that evening at Ford Auditorium. I probably could have made arrangements if I had known a few days in advance. But once I had heard his house had been bombed, I figured he wasn't coming. I had an opportunity but didn't take it. It is a moment that I regret to this day.

Harlem stayed on my mind through the sixties, and though I was miles away in my roost in Detroit, I was as disturbed as Harlemites when the riots raged around them, when the fires raged through dilapidated, unattended buildings, when the drugs eroded the town's foundation, when all but a few die-hards had retreated, leaving the corpse to decay. In 1985, Harlem beckoned again, from an unexpected quarter. My current wife, whom I had known and loved in Detroit, set-tled in Harlem in the early eighties, just a little behind the wave of urban pioneers who were plucking off the valuable but decrepit property and polishing it. By now I was ready for Harlem, ready to stake a claim and determine for myself whether Hughes or Baldwin was right in their descriptions and depictions of the legendary territory, or what little remained of it.

After more than twenty-two years filing stories with the

Amsterdam News as a freelance reporter and writing more than a dozen books, I think I have a feel for Harlem that allows me to speak at least with a modicum of authority. Researching a book on Sugar Ray Robinson, compiling the anthology *The Harlem Reader,* and recently helping a team of writers at the Greater Harlem Chamber of Commerce assemble *Forever Harlem* have been almost as rewarding as the two or three years I spent in close association with the noted historian Dr. John Henrik Clarke. I interviewed Dr. Clarke for articles, covered him at forums, listened to him at rallies, and in the quiet of his library, worked with him on a number of projects and dreamed with him about that definitive book on the history of Harlem. This was so much kindling waiting to be torched when I was approached to do this book. Clarke always expressed great admiration for Baldwin, and believed he revolutionized the essay in the same way Frederick Douglass revolutionized the slave narrative.

I mulled over the idea for a few days, wondering what special perspective I could bring to Baldwin's life and work. There were already several very good biographies, and, even more challenging, Baldwin had pretty much documented his own furious passage in a skein of essays and in what the good reader can decipher from his novels, plays, and poems. But there was not a book that had carefully considered his relationship to Harlem, or how he related to those other significant denizens of the community—Cullen, Hughes, Malcolm X, Conrad Lynn, Harold Cruse, et al.—and the extent to which he had been assailed and enraged by Jews and white liberals in his controversial odyssey.

At bottom, I also felt a pressing need to defend him from some of those writers and critics who seemed to relish bash-

ing him with each new publication, or renouncing him for
being less than totally committed to the struggle for black liberation. I was shocked to read how LeRoi Jones (now Amiri
Baraka), in an essay in 1963, had reduced Baldwin's fervent
plea to nothing more than a "spavined whine" that was "sick-
ening past relief." And then, successively, there were disparaging words from Hughes, Cruse, Eldridge Cleaver, and Stanley
Crouch. Cleaver upset me when he sided with Norman Mailer
over Baldwin, stating how personally insulted he was by
Baldwin's "flippant, schoolmarmish dismissal" of Mailer's
White Negro. For him, Baldwin was filled with self-hatred and
possessed of a "most shameful, fanatical, fawning, sycophan-
tic love of whites." In 1967, about four years after his attack
on Baldwin, Cleaver encountered the writer at a dinner tribute to him in San Francisco. According to Huey Newton, a
leader of the Black Panther Party, Cleaver "bent down and
engaged in a long passionate French kiss with Baldwin." If
this really happened, it was a graphic contradiction of his
merciless attack on Baldwin's homosexuality, or an indication
of his own deep-seated sexual ambivalence. Nowhere in his
essays does Baldwin mention the incident, and it would be a
decade later before he offered any opinion at all of Cleaver,
deeming him something "of a deacon" after meeting him in
Hollywood at the Beverly Hills Hotel.

I was up in arms, too, when Stanley Crouch set out to
crush Baldwin with a passel of inanities, such as indicating
there was "increasing bile and cynicism in his generalized
charges." This was penned a few months after Crouch was
seen elbowing his way into the family cortege during
Baldwin's funeral at the Cathedral of St. John the Divine in
New York. "It was absolutely obscene the way he intruded

into the family line and then wrote that atrocious piece about Baldwin in the *Village Voice*," Quincy Troupe recalled. This was the same Crouch "the contrarian," defined by one friend as "addled by the toxic drug of his terminally inflated ego."

The bouts with Hughes and Cruse will be given greater attention later in this book. Baldwin often chose not to respond to the efforts to demean him; that would be, he once alluded, a way of dignifying the comments, and thereby playing into the hands of his adversaries.

It was when I saw Baldwin pinned against the ropes, and almost nonviolently weathering a barrage of insults from lesser writers, that I was moved to rush to his defense, though I knew full well that he had his own way of retaliating, that special way of transmuting anger into something creative and useful, what Henry Louis Gates, Jr. charitably defined as a "pose of wounded passivity." That's when I wanted to be near him, to register his complaint on whatever frequency he chose to speak and to nurse his damaged ego.

I am still not absolutely sure when I had my moment alone with Baldwin. It was either in September 1976, after attending a fund-raiser for the Mozambique Project, coordinated by Robert Van Lierop, who had just completed his film on the revolution in that country, or it was in the spring of 1978, when Baldwin spoke out against a version of Paul Robeson's life in a one-man performance by James Earl Jones. Both events occurred at Hunter College, and no matter the date, I do remember walking with Baldwin and mainly listening to him. I posed a series of questions to hide my fear of having nothing to say. I'm sure the questions were about as profound as they are memorable now. I was there, either at the suggestion of Van Lierop or Paul Robeson, Jr., to escort him to the house of a friend who lived nearby. There was a slight drizzle that evening and I remember we walked at a very brisk clip. I can remember—like seeing him in pantomime—his hands waving as he talked, a cigarette clutched in his left hand, an ascot puffed about his neck. If we said anything of substance the years have conveniently erased it, and I have a trace of him being there, even as evanescent as Malcolm was in my life.

The Baldwin I have discovered through interviews, with friends and relatives, and his essays and novels is as complex and indefinable as I expected. The story of his life has been a part of the public record for years, and now, fortunately, there are schoolchildren who know the alphabet of his days, the books he wrote, even the places where he lived. But this doesn't make it any easier to grasp his aura. Fitting Baldwin back into his tortuous past had to be done in order to see what I didn't know about him. One of the more rewarding things I learned about him was the strength of his commitment to a cause, or to an individual once he believed in them. Very little has been written about The Harlem Six or Tony Maynard, but Baldwin devoted his time and resources to them with the same unrelenting fervor that he brought to the civil rights movement. Baldwin's passion had a way of illuminating whatever became an issue for him, and it was often the intensity of this involvement that gnawed away at the time he needed to nourish those god-given literary gifts; it is perhaps paradoxical, and this is something that Baldwin probably understood better than anyone else, that the very issues, the fights that sustained him, would ultimately consume him.

While it can't be said that I've discussed definitively

Baldwin's relationship with Cullen, Hughes, Malcolm, and Cruse, these steps should make it a little easier for those who choose to travel behind me. Baldwin blazed a wide and brilliant arc across our intellectual firmament, and so long as we find a way to keep his genius alive and burning there will be a light leading us home, home to *Baldwin's Harlem.*

Chapter 1

BORN IN HARLEM

I was born in Harlem," James Arthur Baldwin declared at the beginning of *Notes of a Native Son,* his first published collection of nonfiction. And he described this location in Harlem as "a very wide avenue" in his essay "Notes for a Hypothetical Novel," where the vicinity was known as "The Hollow." "Now it's called Junkie's Hollow," he added. Most of the junkies of Baldwin's day, whether he was referring to dope addicts or the old men who picked up rags and iron, vanished from the scene a generation ago, subsequently replaced by crack addicts and an urban tribe of hunters and gatherers looking for bottles and cans, and anything else the market would bear. The Harlem Baldwin knew has undergone stages of dramatic change, and the most recent transformation–the incessant advance of gentrification–may soon give Harlem the same demographics that were so evident at the beginning of the twentieth century when various European ethnic groups were among the dominant residents. To some degree, Baldwin anticipated these relative social and political changes, and it might have been the perfect kind of diversified Harlem to appeal to his universal outlook, though one assesses Baldwin's mood and attitude at great risk.

"When I grew up we lived in what was recognized as a neighborhood," Baldwin told anthropologist Margaret Mead during their conversation. "Everybody vaguely knew everybody else. We knew the man who ran the drugstore, the man who ran the butcher shop. We may not have liked all these people, but there they were. Later on, when they started tearing down the slums, as they said, and building these hideous barracks, the neighborhood disappeared. There was no longer communication between the people."

To be sure, whether stated proudly or with disdain, Harlem would be a recurring theme in all of Baldwin's works. In a later chapter, we will see that his native community took on a variety of configurations, sometimes a fully developed character elbowing into conversations, and at other times a shadowy presence, hardly noticeable as the action moves in and around its perimeters of hope and despair. Sometimes it was merely a matter of whether the scenario was real or imagined. Though Baldwin left Harlem when he was nineteen—never to live there again and returning only for occasional visits—he had "absorbed the full impact of the community," said his sister Gloria Karefa-Smart. "He often came back because we were there. But by the time he was a teenager, he had gathered a wealth of experience, much of which can be found in his fiction and nonfiction."

James Baldwin was born on August 2, 1924, in Harlem Hospital. The hospital, which had been founded in 1887 in a brownstone on 120th Street and the East River, was greatly expanded once it was relocated in 1911 to Lenox Avenue between 135th and 137th Streets, about four blocks from the first of several Baldwin residences in Harlem. In 1920, perhaps capitulating to community pressure to employ black doctors, the hospital hired Dr. Louis T. Wright. Dr. Wright arrived six years before Dr. May Chinn was hired as the first African American female intern at the hospital. It was a hot and humid Saturday when Baldwin came screaming into the world, and if he had come a day earlier his wail might have joined the cacophony of trumpets, trombones, and thumping drums from a massive parade of Garveyites that had filed past the hospital on their way to nearby Liberty Hall, next door to Abyssinian Baptist Church on 138th Street, for their annual convention. There was probably enough noise to induce labor. By this time, the flamboyant Marcus Garvey had already been convicted of using the mail to defraud patrons who sought to purchase stock in the financially troubled Black Star Line. By 1925, he would begin serving a sentence that was ended in 1927 when President Calvin Coolidge pardoned him and then had him deported.

"Eight modest, unassuming brass bands blared away down Lenox Avenue," recalled author Zora Neale Hurston. "A few thousand pennants strung across the street overhead . . . a few floats, a dozen or so titled officials and he [Marcus Garvey] was ready for his annual parade." The Universal Negro Improvement Association's monthlong fourth annual International Convention of Negro Peoples of the World was well under way by the time baby Baldwin began to gaze about him, sizing up his surroundings with his alert, all-seeing eyes, and at the same time seeking comfort ever deeper into his mother's embrace. "A black boy born in New York's Harlem in 1924," Baldwin wrote, "was born of southerners who had but lately been driven from land, and therefore was born into a southern community." His mother, Emma Berdis Jones, was twenty-two years old and unmarried. She had arrived in New York City from Deal Island, Maryland, near the mouth of Chesapeake Bay, along with that multitude of migrants, "blues people" from the South who were fleeing Jim Crow, the Klan, and a horde of other social and political demons that made life dangerous and unbearable for many black Americans.

Baldwin had no idea who his birth father was, and thus he wrote hardly anything about him. About Berdis, as she was called, there are only a few places in which she is discussed with more than passing remarks. What he did recall was that his mother, like him and his siblings, lived in dread and fear of David Baldwin, whom she married three years later. "It did not take me long, nor did the children, as they came tumbling into this world, take long to discover that our mother paid an immense price for standing between us and our father," James wrote. Like an usher, the eldest child stood by, seemingly with a counter, noting the arrival of his brothers and sisters: "George in January [1928], Barbara, in August [1929], Wilmer, in October [1930], David, in December [1931], Gloria [1933], Ruth [1935], Elizabeth [1937], and (when we thought it was over!) Paula Maria [1943], named by me, born on the day our father died, all in the summertime." In those days, Baldwin lamented, "My mother was given to the exasperating and mysterious habit of having babies. As they were born, I took them over with one hand and held a book with the other." To date, while all of his sisters are alive and well, only George remains of his brothers.

The one time he described his mother was in a recollection of a childhood day when he came running into the house after seeing an ugly drunk woman on the street, and asked her to hurry to the window to view the hideous creature. "You see? You see? She's uglier than you, Mama! She's uglier than me!" There is no record of his mother's response to this comment, and photos of Berdis indicate that she may not have been a raving beauty, but she was by no means an ugly woman, unless the stylized figure of Eshu of the Yoruba—with its bulging eyes that "embody the power to make things happen"—is unsightly.

Whatever her visage, it was no better or worse than the thousands who flocked with her beyond the "cotton curtain," looking for better opportunities in the so-called northern promised land. "By 1920 the section of Harlem bordered approximately by 130th Street on the south, 145th Street on the north, and west of Fifth Avenue to Eighth Avenue was predominantly Negro—and inhabited by some 73,000 people. Two-thirds of Manhattan's Negro population lived there in 1920," historian Gilbert Osofsky observed. The Baldwins lived within this narrowly circumscribed enclave, never moving beyond these boundaries. They had been there since the pioneering days of Philip Payton, who founded the Afro-Am Realty Company, and the enterprising Lillian Harris "Pig Foot Mary" Dean, who parlayed a business selling chitterlings, roasted corn, and other products into a real estate empire.

Like Pig Foot Mary, Baldwin and his brothers often demonstrated entrepreneurial zeal. "People were doing all kinds of things to make a living, shining shoes, selling papers," George Baldwin recalled. "Me, Lover [Wilmer] and some of our friends would sell firewood to our neighbors. We would get the wood from over on the east side from a lot of abandoned houses. We would carry our axes and bushel baskets and follow behind the WPA [Works Project or Progress Administration] workers, picking up what they had left behind after they finished a job. The heavy thick wood we got would burn longer, so this would be sold to the coal flats."

"Harlem was not an all-black community during the time I was growing up," Baldwin wrote. Among the smorgasbord of ethnicities scattered around Harlem were Italians, Irish, Finns, Poles, Jews, West Indians and other 'exotics.' We could all be found eating as much as we could hold in Father Divine's restaurant for fifteen cents," he recalled, referring to the religious cult leader who provided inexpensive meals for the homeless and destitute during the Depression.

Given the diversity of ethnic groups competing for jobs, housing, and self-respect, the turbulence and conflict among them were inevitable. But for all the talk about racial tension, the main source of discord was between African Americans and the influx of immigrants from the Caribbean. Despite their racial commonality, their differences in culture, religion, and lifestyle often left them at odds, and those toxic moments were not relieved by ridicule, insults, and doggerel hurled at the new arrivals by native blacks and others. "When a monkey chaser dies, you don't need an undertaker, throw him in the Harlem River, and he'll float back to Jamaica" was a common verse, mocking some of the newcomers and often leading to violence. Rudolph Fisher, novelist and short story writer of the Harlem Renaissance, captured some of the tension that resulted from confrontations between indigenous blacks and the influx of people from the islands. His haughty West Indian protagonist, Cyril Sebastian Best, not only looked down his nose at Black Americans but his own kinsmen. "There were British West Indians in Harlem who would have told Cyril Sebastian Best flatly to his face that they despised him—that he would not have dared even address them in the islands; who frequently reproved their American friends for judging all West Indians by the Cyril Sebastian Best standard. There were others who, simply because he was a British West Indian, gathered him to their bosoms in that regardless warmth with which the outsider ever welcomes his like." Thus the dynamic of race relations was not exclusively limited to insults and fights between the islanders and African Americans. The newcomers had their own class, caste color, and style distinctions that often ignited dissension. These factors, along with white flight, created a new demographic in Harlem; the mixture also gave rise to the emergence of the ghetto that would later figure prominently in Baldwin's early essays.

Harlem, which had grown exponentially since the turn of the century, may have been a keg of human dynamite, but one wouldn't have known it from the bustling nightlife. When the Cotton Club opened officially in 1918, it sparked an explosion of other clubs, including Connie's Inn, at 131st and Seventh Avenue, Smalls' Paradise, at 135th and Seventh Avenue, and Leroy's, at 135th Street and Fifth Avenue. The clubs were one way to hold on to the dwindling white residents, particularly when they catered to white patrons only. There were reputed to be more than 125 nightclubs in Harlem by the mid-1920s. However, the jovial nightlife with "slumming" whites perhaps obscured the erosion of the community's infrastructure.

If the storied "Harlem Renaissance" was in full bloom following the success of the Broadway production of *Shuffle Along* in 1921, it was a cultural phenomenon that bypassed most Harlemites struggling to make ends meet. In his writings Baldwin seldom mentioned this glorious era that has gained its own special niche in American history. In "Notes for a Hypothetical Novel," he wrote with a rather dismissive tone that "as I was coming into the world there was something going on called the Negro Renaissance; and the most distinguished survivor of that time is Mr. Langston Hughes. This Negro Renaissance is an elegant term which means that white people had then discovered that Negroes could act and write as well as sing and dance and this Renaissance was not destined to last very long." On several occasions he cited the works of Steinbeck, Dos Passos, Hemingway, Cain, Faulkner, and other white authors of the twenties and thirties; but such Harlem literary stalwarts as Rudolph Fisher, Claude McKay, Zora Neale Hurston, Jean Toomer, Wallace Thurman, W.E.B. Du Bois, Nella Larsen, Dorothy West, Jessie Fauset, Walter White, Carl Van Vechten (one of the few whites able to gain entry in the salons without being charged with "slumming"), and other prominent writers of the period, if mentioned at all, are given short shrift. Van Vechten is given a special nod in the foreword Baldwin wrote for Bobby Seale in 1977, where Baldwin points out that *Nigger Heaven*, Van Vechten's novel, was published around the time of his birth. However, rat- and roach-infested Harlem was hardly a heaven, he recalled. To his credit, though, Baldwin does single out Louis Armstrong, Duke Ellington, and Bessie Smith, among other musicians who are generally ignored in the rapture about the renaissance. Of course, there is nothing startling about this inclusion from Baldwin, for, as he wrote in "Many Thousands Gone," "It is only in his music, which Americans are able to admire because a protective sentimentality limits their understanding of it, that the Negro in America has been able to tell his story." Apparently none of Harlem's writers who preceded him warranted any discussion. Only Countee Cullen and Langston Hughes appear in his essays or reviews, and more will be said about those relationships later.

Certainly one can argue the relative literary merits of any of the above authors and their works, but many of these stories have offered Baldwin and others substantial insight on the Harlem community's morals, values, and ethics, and especially the pervasive racial tension. There is much to be learned about the contest between native blacks of Harlem and their kin from the Caribbean in Fisher's short stories, most notably "Ringtail," and in his novel *The City of Refuge*. From Nella Larsen's *Passing*, Baldwin could have gathered insight into "double consciousness" and the conflict of cultures that resonated at Harlem's social and political core. The works of W.E.B. Du Bois gave the concept added depth and dimension. From *There Is Confusion*, Jessie Fauset's novel (which, like Walter White's *Fire in the Flint*, was published the year of Baldwin's birth), Baldwin could have gleaned a few of the racial and sexual complexities that governed the lives of Harlem's black women, many of them his mother's contemporaries. And in Claude McKay's *Home to Harlem* there is an unrelenting celebration of the lower class, which stands in stark contrast to Baldwin's nonfiction summaries, even as McKay somewhat anticipates Baldwin's fictional portrayals.

There is no way to gauge the impact of the Garvey movement or the Harlem Renaissance on Baldwin, or even the fulminations of the nascent labor activism of A. Philip Randolph and Chandler Own that was disseminated through the pages of the *Messenger*, or the revolutionary tendencies represented by the African Blood Brotherhood that were then vibrating through Harlem. There were certainly remnants of all these things by the time Baldwin was old enough to venture from home and begin his encounters with the community and the world, but it's no easy task to define how these experiences were transmuted through his art—or if they were at all. This is a challenge Baldwin's fiction and nonfiction will show us.

"I hit the streets when I was seven," Baldwin wrote in the opening lines of "Dark Days." "It was the middle of the Depression and I learned how to sing out of hard experience." In 1931, as Baldwin notes, Harlem was not exempt from the throes of the Great Depression, and he must have witnessed, on his way to P.S. 24, located on 128th Street between Fifth Avenue and Madison, the long bread lines snaking through the community. For most black residents of Harlem, save for the well-heeled living on Sugar Hill and Strivers' Row, the Depression only added to the stark, miserable conditions. During several interviews Baldwin remembered these terrible times when he was perpetually hungry, and subsisting on a diet of "corned beef and prunes." "My mother fried corned beef, she boiled, she baked it, she put potatoes in it, she put rice in it, she disguised it in corn bread, she boiled it in soup, she wrapped it in cloth, she beat it with a hammer, she banged it against the wall, she threw it onto the ceiling," Baldwin wrote in "Here Be Dragons."

For all the pains of poverty and starvation, some of Harlem's poor found solace in the fact that their predicament was better than the fate facing the Scottsboro Boys, nine young blacks who had been charged with assault and rape after a melee on a train in northern Alabama that was bound for Memphis, Tennessee. As in many black communities across the nation, large rallies were held in Harlem in the boys' defense. These were mainly organized by the NAACP and the Communist Party, which by this time had attained a respectable reputation in Harlem. Not too far from Baldwin's home on Park Avenue, on April 25, 1931, "Five thousand Harlemites jammed Lenox Avenue near 140th Street to hear Communist speakers, and watched a group of 500 communists, predominantly white, march onto Lenox Avenue without a permit, precipitating a violent clash with police."

The outcry and the protests of the injustice over the Scottsboro Boys were momentary compared to the broad political unrest voiced by speakers on the corners of many of Harlem's streets. Rarely in Baldwin's writings is there mention of the street orators who assailed racism and white supremacy or advocated socialism and Black Nationalism. But given their visibility and activism, it was hard to ignore them. There were bitter denunciations from such activists as Cyril Briggs, W. A. Domingo, Grace Campbell, Claudia Jones, Harry Haywood, Hubert Harrison, and the redoubtable Richard B. Moore, who had also worked tirelessly in the campaign to free the Scottsboro Boys. These voices also wailed against the dire economic circumstances so graphically described by Anna Arnold Hedgeman, then secretary of the West 137th Street Branch of the YWCA and often a volunteer in soup kitchens: "A large mass of Negroes was faced with the reality of starvation and they turned sadly to public relief. A few chanted optimistically, 'Jesus will lead me, and Welfare will feed me.' Meanwhile men, women and children searched in garbage cans for food, foraging with dogs and cats." Too many denizens of Harlem, she said, were "packed in damp, rat-ridden dungeons, [and] they existed in squalor not too different from that of the Arkansas sharecroppers." The Depression had come, and most Harlemites didn't know the difference.

Baldwin later confessed that he knew nothing of the political beliefs of his teachers at P.S. 24, but he also stated that "some of the white teachers were very definitely on the Left. They opposed Franco's Spain and Mussolini's Italy and Hitler's Third Reich. For these extreme opinions, several were placed on blacklists and drummed out of the academic community–to the everlasting shame of that community." This is clearly Baldwin's reflection on an earlier stage of his life, and, curiously, the time frame does not exactly fit his first years at elementary school, though it certainly falls within the five years that witnessed the eruption and spread of fascism. Of the black teachers at the school–and again we must presume he's talking about P.S. 24–they were "laconic about politics but single-minded about the future of black students." Many of them, he noted, "were survivors of the Harlem Renaissance and wanted us black students to know that we could do, become anything."

Among this caring coterie of teachers was Gertrude E. Ayer, the school's principal, and the first black principal in the history of New York City schools. (Baldwin mistakenly remembered her as Ayers; her surname was Ayer.) Baldwin recalled her brilliance and her achievements, but said nothing more about her. To be sure, Gertrude Elise Ayer (née Johnson) was a pioneering educator, but she was also a proficient writer and feminist. Born October 13, 1884, in New York City, Ayer came from a very successful family. Her father, Peter Augustus Johnson, was the third black American admitted to practice medicine in New York City. Her mother was English and an expert needlewoman. Ayer married Cornelius W. McDougald in 1911, after completing studies at Hunter College, Columbia University, City College, and New York University. Her husband was the initial counsel for Marcus Garvey during his trial for mail fraud in 1923 (though, for the most part, Garvey was his own lawyer). Later, he was appointed United States assistant district attorney. While her husband was defending Garvey, Ayer, a sprightly, very attractive light-skinned woman, was in the nation's capital delivering a speech on the necessity of education and vocation for African Americans. "Education is on the increase—and the Negro must get his just share," she declared. "Industry is becoming more humanized—the Negro must be regarded in the new light."

In 1924, Ayer passed a competitive exam and was appointed an assistant principal at P.S. 89 in Manhattan. One of the noteworthy students under her tutelage during this phase was Olivia Pearl Stokes (1916–2002), later to become the first African American woman to receive a doctorate in religious education. Without a college degree, Ayer herself became the first black woman to hold a principalship in New York City public schools, in February 1935, by which time Baldwin was eleven years old. Ten years later, in 1945, she was appointed the principal at P.S. 119, where she would remain until her retirement in 1954. Along with her educational duties, Ayer was a member of a number of social and political organizations, including Alpha Kappa Alpha Sorority. She was eighty when she died on July 10, 1971.

Baldwin was just one of many admirers and beneficiaries of Ayer's indomitable spirit. And her young charges must sometimes have felt her firm guidance and been inspired by her resolute stance, especially her encouraging words to the women and the black girls of Harlem. "In New York City," she wrote, "nearly three hundred Negro women share the good conditions in the teaching profession. They measure up to the high pedagogical requirements of the city and state law and are increasingly, leaders in the community." "I loved and feared the lady–for she really was a lady, and a great one–with that trembling passion only twelve year olds can feel," Baldwin told David Leeming. And years later she still remembered Baldwin, as a "very slim, small boy with that haunted look."

Some of the teachers under Ayer's stewardship may not have viewed Baldwin as haunted, but they did immediately recognize the intelligence of their aspiring protégé. Within months of entering P.S. 24, Baldwin earned the attention of Orilla Miller, whom Baldwin would dub "Bill." She had arrived in New York after finishing Antioch College in 1933. A year later, as part of the WPA, she conducted theater educational programs and P.S. 24 was one of the schools on her schedule. Bill was a beautiful woman, Baldwin recalled, and because of her "I never really managed to hate white people."

Bill Miller took the impressionable Baldwin under her liberal wing, and he wrote fondly of her and at length in *The*

Devil Finds Work. "She didn't baffle me," he said, the way some white landlords and storekeepers had, "and she never frightened me and never lied to me. I never felt her pity, either, in spite of the fact that she sometimes brought us old clothes (because she worried about our winters) and cod-liver oil, especially for me, because I seemed destined, then, to be carried away by whooping cough." She didn't call him a nigger; in fact she herself "was treated like a nigger, especially by the cops." It was Miller who introduced him to the world of film, where he first saw the "frog eyes" of Bette Davis, which somewhat relieved the stigma and the stinging insults he had experienced daily from friends and foes who saw him as "strange." If Davis could make it in Hollywood, then maybe there was hope for him, too; maybe his strangeness would not be a handicap to success.

Miller also took Baldwin to plays and even helped to stage and direct the first play he had written. Baldwin retained fervent memories of the time Miller and her sister took him to the Lafayette Theater on Seventh Avenue between 131st and 132nd Streets, near Connie's Inn and the legendary Tree of Hope, which performers often touched for good luck, to see an all-black voodoo version of *Macbeth* produced by Orson Welles and starring Canada Lee. Opening night was April 14, 1936, and the turnout was massive, with theatergoers clogging the streets and sidewalks for blocks in every direction. Along with the prospect of making money, and entertaining a community still recovering from the ravages of a race riot that had left shards of property damage, there was a hope that the production would help revive black theater in Harlem, which theater had suffered serious setbacks since the late twenties.

For the most part, critics, particularly those opposed to WPA projects, weren't sure what to make of the production. Percy Hammond of the *New York Herald Tribune* summed it up as an "exhibition of deluxe boondoggling . . . an ostentatious spectacle," and expressed exasperation at the waste of taxpayers' money. As Wendy Smith notes, "When Hammond died suddenly a few days later, a rumor circulated among the [Federal Theatre Project] Negro Unit staff that he was the victim of malevolent spells cast by the enraged voodoo drummers." It was reminiscent of the judge dropping dead after sentencing Father Divine to prison.

As for Baldwin's assessment of the play, he later wrote that Shakespeare had only a minimal effect on him back then, though according to Miller he was clearly mesmerized. The Bard's intimidation would occur further down the road—but Miller had achieved her purpose of having him see a play with an all-black cast. "The play ran for ten weeks at the Lafayette with sixty-four sold out shows," wrote Mona Z. Smith. "On 'Relief Nights,' seats sold for as little as five cents, a price that encouraged many to see a play for the first time in their lives." In his book *The Crisis of the Negro Intellectual*, Harold Cruse pointed out that Baldwin had "garbled Harlem's theatrical history" during an interview with the *Herald Tribune* in 1964 by confusing the Lafayette Players (a Negro repertory company organized well before World War I by Anita Bush, with Clarence Muse and Dooley Wilson among its illustrious alumni) with the Lafayette Theater. But Baldwin may have been right since Bush moved her group from the Lincoln Theater to the Lafayette, which brought about the change of name. Cruse went on to excoriate Baldwin on several other counts that had no pertinence to the issue at hand. It would be the first of many bitter encounters between them that we will examine extensively in a later chapter.

Eventually the Lafayette—like so many of the theaters that depended on stage productions—switched to showing movies, and by 1950, five years before Baldwin completed *The Amen Corner,* it was converted to a church. It is currently the Williams Christian Methodist Church. A New Lafayette Theater would emerge for a brief spell in 1968, under the aegis of playwright Ed Bullins and director Robert Macbeth. Gordon Polatnick, owner of the Big Apple Jazz Club and Café, directly across the street from that historic site, dreams of restoring that vista. "And I would put the Tree of Hope right back where it used to be," he said.

Baldwin was ten years old when a riot ripped Harlem apart in the spring of 1935. If he knew the details of the incident, they were not revealed in any of his works, though he must have heard about it in the streets, at home, and through the sermons of the Reverend Adam Clayton Powell, Jr. at Abyssinian Baptist Church, where Baldwin and his family were members. Months before the riot, the Harlem streets were abuzz with the protests and demonstrations led by Powell against department stores where blacks were not employed. His retinue was armed with placards that proclaimed "Don't Buy Where You Can't Work!" Powell also rushed to the defense of families who had been evicted from their homes, taking his cue from the Communist Party, which had earlier begun a similar action. "I would walk the streets looking for an evicted family," Powell explained in his autobiography, "and when I found one, I immediately sent a protest committee to the owner of the building, saying 'Put that family back in their home or we will have every family in the building refuse to pay their rent.'" It appears that at no time were the Baldwins threatened with eviction, but without the extra income brought home by Baldwin and his brother George from "shining shoes and selling shopping bags," their mother's meager wages from cleaning "white ladies' apartments" would not have been enough to hold off the avaricious landlords. As the breadwinner, David Baldwin was a common laborer, menially employed at a distant job on Long Island where he worked at a soda bottling plant; he also earned a few dollars from the collection box as a storefront preacher with a tiny congregation. Baldwin said that when he was growing up his stepfather never made more than $27.50 a week.

"My family lived on Park Avenue, just above the uptown railroad tracks," Baldwin observed. "The poverty of my childhood differed from the poverty of today [this was written in 1980] in that the TV set was not sitting in front of our faces, forcing us to make unbearable comparisons between the room we were sitting in and the rooms we were watching, neither were we endlessly being told what to wear and drink and buy. We knew that we were poor, but then, everybody around us was poor." Poverty and police brutality were the twin demons that menaced Harlem when Lino Rivera, a Puerto Rican youth of sixteen, was arrested and accused of shoplifting at S. H. Kress on 125th Street and Lenox Avenue. His arrest triggered rumors that he had been beaten to death in the store's basement. As historian Herbert Shapiro writes, "The incident at the store itself symbolized two elements of the explosive situation, the white-owned retail establishment that was located in the black community and yet refused to hire black clerks, and the police who often enough had given evidence that they were quite capable of the excess use of force." This was not a clash between races, but an attack upon property, though James Thompson, nineteen, was killed after being shot in the chest by a detective while looting a store. More than two hundred stores had their windows broken and were looted, according to police reports. Mayor Fiorello LaGuardia called the disturbance an "unfortunate occurrence" and said it was "instigated and artificially stimulated by a few irresponsible individuals."

The mayor quickly named a committee, including A. Philip Randolph of the Sleeping Car Porters; Hubert Delaney, a prominent Harlemite and the city's tax commissioner; and the poet Countee Cullen, who was also a teacher at Frederick Douglass Junior High School, where Baldwin had recently enrolled. Mayor LaGuardia also placed some of the blame on the Communist Party, which he accused of inciting the riot with its fliers full of false statements about police brutality. In a counterstatement, James Ford, a ranking African American of the Communist Party, said the cause was the starvation conditions and the suffering of Harlem Negroes. Others in the community believed that widespread price-gouging by heartless landlords who discriminated against blacks was a key factor. One activist in the tenants association protesting the hikes said her renting agent had refused to accept her $22 rent money, demanding that she pay the entire month's rent of $48, plus $3 for the cost of serving eviction papers. A year and a half after the incident, the mayor's commission released its report, which was published in the *Amsterdam News* in the summer of 1936, not long after *Voodoo Macbeth* had completed its run at the Lafayette. Among the recommendations were the elimination of discrimination against blacks in employment, improvements of relief and health care services at Harlem Hospital, the construction of new schools, and the expansion of recreational facilities. There was also a demand for better housing. "The tenements people were once so proud of are now rather dangerous firetraps and should be rebuilt," a twelve-year-old Baldwin wrote in a school assignment shortly after the mayor's report was released. "There has been some effort on the part of the Housing Authorities to improve them, but as yet they have only operated in a very small field. Now we, who are interested in Harlem, hope that the future will bring a steady growth and improvement."

Harlem's economic development may have been sluggish, moving along in fits and starts, but Baldwin was maturing steadily. The concise prose in "Harlem–Then and Now" provides solid evidence of this. Baldwin's math teacher, Harvard graduate Herman W. Porter, also known as Bill, or "Mr. Discipline," assigned the story and insisted on serious research. "Porter took me downtown to the main branch of the public library at Forty-second Street and waited for me while I began my research," Baldwin recounted. "He was very proud of the story I eventually turned in. But I was so terrified that afternoon that I vomited all over his shoes in the subway." Some of Baldwin's nausea and trauma might have been the result of the earlier encounter between his father and Porter. Porter had arrived at the Baldwins' apartment at 2171 Fifth Avenue to escort him to the library. He was simply astounded by the clutter and noise that greeted him there. No less startling was the presence of David Baldwin, who viewed Porter

as an intruder. With Baldwin's mother hovering in the background over her brood of children, his father let Porter know
in no uncertain terms that he was an unwelcome guest, an
invader. Porter told Fern Marja Eckman that he was relieved
when they finally departed for the library.

Porter guided the young Baldwin to the librarian, gave
him carfare for the return trip home, and left him to do the
research. "I'm sure that was the first time he'd ever seen that
library," Porter said, "and yet he turned in a superb job–
really, a superb job."

Completing the quartet of early Baldwin mentors that
included Ayer, Miller, and Porter was the Harlem Renaissance immortal Countee Cullen.

Chapter 2

ENCOUNTERING COUNTEE CULLEN

By the time Baldwin set foot in Countee Cullen's French classroom at Frederick Douglass Junior High School in 1936, he was twelve and the Harlem Renaissance, in which Cullen was a significant luminary, had run its course. The heyday of artistic explosion, which lasted for fourteen years according to a few cultural critics of the era, endured a number of telling blows before it finally came to an end, collapsing of its own inertia. If the renaissance was "artificial and overreaching," as one historian concluded, it lingered, despite suffering a terrible setback with the sudden death of A'Lelia Walker in August 1931. As the daughter of Madam C. J. Walker, who had made millions with beauty and health products for black women, she was among the most endowed patrons of the arts, often hosting soirees at the "Dark Tower," her salon on 136th Street and Lenox, a space currently occupied by the Countee Cullen Library. Three years later, two of the era's irreplaceable prime movers, writers Rudolph Fisher and Wallace Thurman, died.

These losses, combined with the Great Depression, the Harlem riot of 1935, the departure of such notables as James Weldon Johnson, W.E.B. Du Bois, and Charles Johnson from Harlem, and the shift of their organizational journals from art to politics, left what remained of the renaissance and its aspirations in tatters. The publication of Zora Neale Hurston's *Jonah's Gourd Vine* in 1934 and the return of the illustrious Claude McKay to Harlem that same year were not enough to counter the debilitating political, cultural, and economic factors.

Baldwin and Cullen, whether they acknowledged it or not, had several important things in common: they both considered themselves less than attractive, were homosexuals, were writers (although "not just Negro writers"), attended the same school, and were the "adopted sons" of fundamentalist preachers. Whether Cullen was born in Harlem, like Baldwin, is still debated by scholars. Cullen claimed he was born in New York City, but his college transcript at New York University, dated 1922, lists Lexington, Kentucky, as his place of birth. Equally mysterious is who Cullen's natural parents were and when the Reverend Frederick Asbury Cullen, a notable Harlemite and pastor of Salem Methodist Episcopal Church, adopted him. (Several authorities list the adoption date as 1914.) A native of Maryland, like Baldwin's mother, Reverend Cullen arrived in New York City in 1902, having served two years as a minister at churches in the Baltimore area. In 1924, Reverend Cullen's church had a membership of over 2,500; it had grown considerably, from only three members twenty years earlier. In the same year his adopted son, Countee, published his poem "The Ballad of the Brown Girl," which was the springboard the son needed for publication of his first book, *Color*, in 1925. A closing couplet of his poem "Yet Do I Marvel," which opens the book, is often cited and did more than anything to immortalize him:

> *Yet do I marvel at this curious thing:*
> *To make a poet black, and bid him sing.*

After graduating from New York University, Cullen was accepted at Harvard, where he strode across campus often proudly displaying his Phi Beta Kappa key. Within a year he had his master of arts degree. Given his success as a student and the additional prominence gained from his poetry, Cullen was eagerly sought as a teacher by black colleges and universities. He received his certificate from the New York Board of Education in the winter of 1931, which qualified him to teach French at the junior high school level. Sometime during the next three years, he secured a position at P.S. 139—Frederick Douglass Junior High School—perhaps arriving there a year before Baldwin enrolled.

The circumstances under which Baldwin and Cullen met have been discussed in all the major biographies, but not extensively. Most agree that Cullen taught French to Baldwin and that they were united on the *Douglass Pilot*, where Cullen was either the faculty advisor to the publication or to the literary club, depending on the source. (In *The Evidence of Things Not Seen*, Baldwin notes that Jessie Fauset was one of his teachers, apparently at DeWitt Clinton, for French. Fauset, another writer of prestige from the Harlem Renaissance era, taught at DeWitt Clinton from 1927 to 1944.) Sources also differ on Cullen's impact on Baldwin.

David Leeming writes that it was Cullen who planted the first seeds in Baldwin's mind about going to France; on the other hand, according to James Campbell, there were times when Baldwin could hardly remember the classes he took with Cullen. These differences may derive from Baldwin's selective memory, or even his evasiveness on the issue, a matter briefly touched on by Fern Eckman. That evasiveness is evident in a 1963 interview with psychologist Kenneth B. Clark, himself a graduate of P.S. 139, located then at West 140th Street. Pressed to discuss his years at P.S. 24 and P.S. 139, Baldwin showed reluctance, quickly moving on to the next topic. It becomes obvious that he was not excited by the fact that he and Clark were alumni of the junior high school. (Harold Cruse also attended Frederick Douglass, eight years before Baldwin, and would become a stern critic of his writings.) "I didn't like lot of my teachers, but I had a couple of teachers who were nice to me—one was a Negro teacher," Baldwin noted without naming them. Since both Cullen and Herman Porter were black, it's not clear what is not being said here. He later refers to one of the teachers as being "a little bit colored and little bit white," which may have been his conflation of the years at P.S. 139 with P.S. 24 and the influence of principal Gertrude Ayer, who was of light complexion.

Baldwin's selective memory may have been at work as soon as he left junior high school. When he was a senior at DeWitt Clinton High School in the Bronx, he interviewed Cullen, and, curiously, never mentioned that the poet had been his teacher. He couldn't have known at that time that Cullen was the adopted son of Reverend Cullen, and he was obviously not sure where the minister's church was since he gave it a wrong location. The assignment was for the *Magpie,* the school's literary journal, and that he chose Cullen as his subject was logical since Cullen lived in Harlem and was a famous poet. Moreover, Cullen had also attended DeWitt Clinton. In fact, it was while he was a student there that he published "Life's Rendezvous," one of his earliest poems. That it appeared in the *Magpie* might have been another inducement leading Baldwin to obtain the interview. Already Baldwin was armed with an impressive vocabulary and precision with words. Present, too, was the probing insight, the budding intelligence that even at eighteen presaged the ever-questing writer he would become.

"Asking Mr. Cullen, as per custom, for some secret of success, I was told 'There is no secret to success except hard work and getting something indefinable which we call the "breaks." In order for a writer to succeed, I suggest three things—read and write—and wait,'" Baldwin wrote toward the end of the interview. Then he asked Cullen if he had found much prejudice against blacks in the literary world. The poet told him no. "In this field one gets pretty much what he deserves. . . . If you're really something, nothing can hold you back. In the artistic field, society recognizes the Negro as an equal and, in some cases, as a superior member. When one considers the social and political plights of the Negro today, that is, indeed, an encouraging sign."

It wasn't a very long interview, but Baldwin had done his homework on his former teacher, citing a number of his achievements as a poet. What he knew at eighteen of Cullen, and especially his impact on him, was apparently forgotten or deliberately downplayed by 1984 during an interview with Julius Lester. Consistent with his remarks to James Campbell, Baldwin told Lester that he knew of only two writers of the Harlem Renaissance, Hughes and Cullen, "but for some reason they did not attract me." He was not putting the writers down, he told Lester, "but the world they were describing had nothing to do with me, at that time in my life. Later on I realized something else, but then their work did not resound to me." Baldwin's comments to Lester may have stemmed from a lingering class bias that often surfaced in his writings and interviews, particularly at a time in his life when he tended to identify more with the lower or working class. Earlier in the interview with Lester he had discussed his background and stressed that he came from the Hollow, and not Sugar Hill, where the black middle class predominated. "You see," Baldwin told Lester, "there were two Harlems. Those who lived in Sugar Hill and there was the Hollow, where we lived. There was a great divide between the black people on the Hill and us. I was just a ragged, funny black shoeshine boy, and I was afraid of the people on the Hill, who, for their part, didn't want to have anything to do with me."

That area called Sugar Hill that Baldwin feared overlooked central Harlem, sweeping north from the Gothic tower at Shepherd Hall on the campus at City College to the prestigious residence of 409 Edgecombe, where such prosperous citizens as pioneering Dr. May Chinn, painter Aaron Douglas, classical singer Jules Bledsoe, and NAACP stalwarts W.E.B. Du Bois, Walter White, and Roy Wilkins all lived at one time or another from the 1920s through the 1950s. "Its row of brick and granite apartment houses, with colorful canopies stretching from doorways to sidewalks, are the homes of the upper class and café society," explained author and journalist Roi Ottley, himself a native Harlemite and well acquainted with the Hill's hoi polloi. "The most imposing of these buildings are the twelve-storied Colonial Parkway Apartments [409 Edgecombe] and the Roger Morris Apartments [555 Edgecombe], with smartly uniformed elevator operators and doormen." To include 555 Edgecombe, which is located at 160th Street, Ottley goes five blocks beyond the northern border of Harlem, though this boundary, now designated within the district of Washington Heights, has always varied from generation to generation. By the 1960s, even the Audubon Ballroom, where Malcolm X was assassinated, near what is now called New York–Presbyterian Hospital at Broadway and 165th Street, was often considered part of Harlem.

Ottley doesn't mention Hamilton Terrace, a very luxurious section of the Hill and quite comparable to the elite Strivers' Row. Named after Alexander Hamilton, whose summer home, Hamilton Grange, was built in 1802 and moved down Convent Avenue from 143rd Street, the area still draws a daily bevy of tourists. Baldwin's distaste for the people on the Hill perhaps didn't extend to Cullen, who at one time resided at 317 Convent Avenue, next door to Billy Strayhorn, composer of the Duke Ellington classic "Take the 'A' Train." Nor did Ottley discuss how Sugar Hill got its name. It may have come from the notion that residents were living the "sweet life," or from the musical comedy *Sugar Hill* written by Charles Tazewell in 1931. Done in blackface and with music composed by Flournoy Miller and Aubrey Lyles, of *Shuffle Along* fame, it lasted only eleven performances.

The closest Baldwin may have gotten to Sugar Hill, which was far across town from his home and school, was in his imagination. During his senior year at P.S. 139, by now the editor in chief of the *Pilot*, he wrote a sketch called "One Sunday Afternoon." All the action between an inquiring character, clearly Baldwin, and a tramp down on his luck takes place in St. Nicholas Park, stretched below the cliffs of Sugar Hill. It's a sentimental, cautionary tale that is most memorable for a declaration, if not a credo, from the thirteen-year-old aspiring playwright. Why does he want to be a writer? the tramp asked him. "Well, I'm very good at English," Baldwin responds, "and I've written quite a number of plays in school, and everyone seems to think I have talent. I'm willing to work very hard in order to succeed."

It is not clear whether Baldwin ever took an English class from Cullen. Even so, given the teacher's role as an advisor to the literary club and in helping to oversee the *Pilot* and its writers, the two must have found time to discuss a number of things about literature and aspirations. And if one noted Baldwin authority is correct, Cullen shared with Baldwin and his other students portions of his escapades in Paris. In his biography of Baldwin, David Leeming said Baldwin told him that "his dream of going to France originated with Cullen." According to Eckman, this assertion was corroborated years later in a letter Baldwin wrote to Cullen's widow conveying his indebtedness to Cullen. Of course, there is the possibility that Baldwin's sojourn in Paris was influenced by Richard Wright, who had befriended him before moving to Europe himself in 1947. Leeming elaborated on the closeness between Baldwin and Cullen. "There was a less tangible rapport that he spoke of—a comforting sense that Cullen and he instinctively understood something about each other, something that prepubescent inexperience would have made impossible for Baldwin to identify then

as homosexuality," he wrote. "Countee Cullen was everything that Jimmy's stepfather was not—a warm man, one
who was not afraid to touch, who entered into his students'
lives."

If nothing more than from a literary intrusion, Cullen certainly entered into Baldwin's life, deeply influencing his poetic
dreams. Baldwin's first efforts as a poet were almost exact imi-
tations of Cullen's style. Later, however, as Baldwin sought to
find his own style, he gave his teacher one of his poems to critique. The poem was called "Black Girl Shouting."

> *Black girl, whirl*
> *Your torn, red dress. Black girl, hide*
> *Your bitterness. Black girl, stretch*
> *Your mouth so wide. None will guess*
> *The way he died.*

Cullen's only remark: "It's an awful lot like Hughes," meaning of course Langston Hughes, whose style, according to
Ted Gottfried, didn't appeal to Cullen. (Apparently Cullen's
dislike of Hughes's poetic voice was not enough to repel him
from seeking the latter's assistance prior to his first voyage to
Paris.) Cullen may have not only dampened Baldwin's enthusiasm to write poetry, as Gottfried contends, he may have
also unwittingly prejudiced him against Hughes. If so, such
an attitude did not come right away, since as early as 1948
Hughes had written to Baldwin praising his essay "The
Harlem Ghetto." For Hughes, Baldwin's conclusions about
their common community was "a most beautifully written
and effective" piece. Five years later the esteemed poet would
weigh in again, congratulating Baldwin for his "Everybody's

Protest Novel," which was among three lengthy essays he crafted to denounce the social realism school of writing, or protest fiction, best exemplified by Richard Wright.

When Baldwin was mulling which high school he should attend, it was Cullen who recommended that he consider DeWitt Clinton in the Bronx, from which Cullen graduated. "At that time Clinton was among the top-rated schools in New York City," Gottfried writes. "Clinton graduates include Richard Rodgers and Fats Waller, Charles Rangel, and Neil Simon, Burt Lancaster and Nate Archibald, and many other high achievers. With Cullen's recommendation James Baldwin was accepted to Clinton."

Now, for the first time in his young life, Baldwin would be stepping beyond a familiar terrain, but his teachers had armed him with all the love and sophistication needed to excel at the next plateau.

Chapter 3

Langston Hughes

It's not clear exactly when Baldwin became aware of Langston Hughes, but the great writer's reputation might have first loomed over Baldwin when his teacher Countee Cullen said that Baldwin's poetry reminded him of Hughes's style. From that, Baldwin said, "I stopped writing poetry." For some unknown reason, Baldwin, then about twelve years old, was not flattered by Cullen's critique. To be compared to Hughes, who by this time was thirty-two and had been famous since he was a teenager with his poem "The Negro Speaks of Rivers," would have struck most aspiring writers as a compliment, rather than a rebuke. It might have been Cullen's tone or the way he said what he said that made Baldwin reject Hughes. In any case, instead of being turned on, Baldwin tuned out.

Baldwin doesn't mention Hughes in his stunning essay "The Harlem Ghetto," which appeared in *Commentary* in 1948 when he was twenty-four years old. Given the focus of the essay, the omission of Hughes is nothing to harp on, but Baldwin does mention Lena Horne, Paul Robeson, Chester

Himes, Richard Wright, and even George Schuyler, a writer who shared many moments with Hughes during the storied Harlem Renaissance. Hughes, as Baldwin recounted in his "The Role of the Writer in America," written in 1960, was the lone survivor of that era that he knew, but Baldwin may have disdainfully lumped the poet with the "folks who lived on Sugar Hill," where Hughes lived before settling into Harlem's valley or "Hollow" in his later years. In an interview with Julius Lester, Baldwin stated that he knew of Hughes's and Cullen's work, but found neither to his liking. He said their work "did not resound to me," and moreover, "The Black middle class was essentially an abstraction to me." This phrase would come back to haunt him in the hands of Harold Cruse.

Much of this distaste for Hughes was probably born more of shyness than in a general dislike for the bourgeoisie. It also might have been merely the emerging, tormented young writer tossed between admiration and envy. In this state of mixed feelings, Baldwin idolized Hughes yet also possibly sought to replace him—to "slay him," as he was later said to have done in a literary way to Richard Wright. Depending on who was conducting an interview and when, Baldwin either didn't live that far from Hughes or he was far away; whether near or far, it never occurred to him to reach out to the literary giant. He perhaps chose to make it on his own merits.

Hughes apparently first gave notice to Baldwin when he sent him a letter after the publication of Baldwin's article on the Harlem ghetto in *Commentary* in 1948. Hughes was probably made aware of the article by his friend Arna Bontemps, with whom he would share a life of correspondence. Bontemps showered accolades on Baldwin: "He has zoomed high among our writers with his first effort." As for the content of Hughes's letter, it remains a mystery, though given Bontemps' lavish praise, it must have been at least momentarily commendatory. Only years later did Baldwin explain why he never replied. "I just didn't know what to say. So, I didn't say anything." Baldwin's reticence, his failure to respond to Hughes, is in one way uncharacteristic of Baldwin, who by this time had often expressed an aggressive attitude on the literary terrain. Whether praised or dismissed, Baldwin never let on about what Hughes had to say.

From 1948 to 1954, Baldwin lived in France and Switzerland. This separation from America, its culture, and particularly its literature, put him in touch with European masters, artifacts, and edifices–"Dante, Shakespeare, Michelangelo, Aeschylus, Da Vinci, Rembrandt, Racine . . . the cathedral at Chartres." For contact with his Afro-American past he relied on the records of Bessie Smith and Fats Waller, both of whom he enjoyed in defiance of his father, who despised and had forbidden such music in his home.

Baldwin returned from Europe in the middle of the McCarthy witch hunts, which made life miserable for anyone perceived as even having an anti-American thought. Baldwin's visit was timed with the 1953 publication of his first novel, *Go Tell It on the Mountain.* The reviews were mixed. One critic compared Baldwin with Faulkner, which must have made Baldwin smile and cringe at the same time, while others felt the work was burdened with "excessive" diction and lacked the bravura of Ralph Ellison's *Invisible Man.* But one of the most stinging assessments came from Hughes.

Hughes had initially praised the book, perhaps having

read only a few chapters. But several days after receiving the book he had a different impression. In a letter to Bontemps, Hughes compared Baldwin not with Faulkner but with Zora Neale Hurston, with whom he had feuded after a failed collaboration back in the 1930s. He contended that Baldwin "over-writes and over-poeticizes in images way over the heads of the folks supposedly thinking them." The book, he concluded, was "a low-down story in a velvet bag." To some extent this slap was a continuation of their disagreement on the merits of Harriet Beecher Stowe's *Uncle Tom's Cabin,* which Hughes had praised and Baldwin had excoriated.

Nevertheless, Hughes forwarded a promised blurb to Knopf, the same publisher who had all but canceled his contract with the company. In a rather disingenuous way, Hughes wrote, "He is thought-provoking, tantalizing, irritating, abusing and amusing. And he uses words as the sea uses waves, to flow and beat, advance and retreat, rise and take a bow in disappearing . . . the thought becomes poetry and the poetry illuminates the thought." A blurb in one place gave way to a blast in another when Hughes, three years later, assailed Baldwin, letting him know of his preference for *Notes of a Native Son* over *Go Tell It on the Mountain.* Still, this preference is almost as barbed as his remarks on the novel. "That Baldwin's viewpoints are half American, half Afro-American, incompletely fused, is a hurdle which Baldwin himself realizes he still has to surmount," Hughes asserted. "When he does, there will be a straight-from-the-shoulder writer, writing about the troubled problems of this troubled earth with an illuminating intensity that should influence for the better all who ponder on the things books say." In other words, Baldwin was a promising writer, but still had a long way to go. Hughes's incomparable biographer, Arnold Rampersad, summed up the growing chasm between them: "an unfortunate and unbridgeable gap had opened between Langston and the most gifted new black writer." Baldwin did not wait long to retaliate. Baldwin accepted an offer to review *Selected Poems* in 1959, in the same pages of the *New York Times Book Review* where Hughes had jumped him three years before. "Every time I read Langston Hughes I am amazed all over again by his genuine gifts—and depressed that he has done so little with them. A real discussion of his work demands more space than I have here, but this book contains a great deal which a more disciplined poet would have thrown into the waste-basket (almost all of the last section, for example)." And that was only Baldwin's opening paragraph; in just a few places did his attack slacken.

Baldwin's dislike for the book's last section shows he was not very excited by Hughes's theme of freedom. It also amounts, quite inexplicably, to the dismissal of two of Hughes's most famous and anthologized poems: "I, Too, Sing America" and "The Negro Mother." As if Countee Cullen were advising him, Baldwin was particularly dismissive of Hughes's "The Weary Blues," which, to his estimation, copied rather than strove to exploit the cadence of the blues. "Hughes," Baldwin wrote, "is an American Negro poet and has no choice but to be acutely aware of it. He is not the first American Negro to find the war between his social and artistic responsibilities all but irreconcilable." Such would not be a dilemma for Paul Robeson, a friend whom Baldwin held in high esteem. "The artist must elect to fight for freedom or for slavery. I have made my choice. I had no alternative," Robeson had announced in 1937. Twenty years later, in 1957, after the civil rights movement gained momentum, Baldwin made his choice, joining the ranks of freedom fighters, a choice many believe affected his writing.

Hughes had used the metaphor of a wave in praising elements of Baldwin's work, and Baldwin returned it in kind, noting "Wave of sorrow/do not drown me now," the opening lines to Hughes's poem "Island." However, the vitriol outweighed the kudos. Baldwin said there were poems "which almost succeed but which do not succeed, poems which take refuge, finally, in a fake simplicity in order to avoid the very difficult simplicity of the experience!" More than one writer, including playwright Lorraine Hansberry, a friend to both men, recognized the lack of respect between them.

Ironically, Hughes had purchased his first house in Harlem, a brownstone at 20 East 127th Street, in the summer of 1948 and was settling in just as Baldwin was preparing to leave. The house was (and is) located almost directly in back of P.S. 29, where Baldwin first matriculated and in the same neighborhood where he spent most of his early youth. Hughes wanted to live right in the vortex of "old Harlem" and the house was perfectly suited to satisfy this quest.

In the winter of that same year, on November 11, Armistice Day, Baldwin had left Harlem for France. This was his farewell departure from the community of his birth and he would never live there again. Except for visits with friends and family, occasional speeches, and attendance at major events, Baldwin relegated Harlem to his essays and novels. And as we will see later, Harlem was treated variously there, though generally with neglect.

Baldwin and Hughes differed vehemently on Harlem, a

place that had been like a second skin to Baldwin during his early years, and one Hughes had embraced with reverence toward the end of his life.

Baldwin's first significant essay, "The Harlem Ghetto," published before his departure to Paris, had slammed the home village as poverty-stricken, overcrowded, sinister, and infested with human and nonhuman vermin. "All of Harlem," Baldwin insisted, "is pervaded by sense of congestion, rather like the insistent, maddening, claustrophobic pounding in the skull that comes from trying to breathe in a very small room with all the windows shut."

Hughes offered a different impression. Yes, Harlem was congested—"congested with people," Hughes cheerfully exclaimed in an appearance on a WABC television program in 1960. "All kinds. And I'm lucky enough to call a great many of them my friends." As if to emphasize his point about Harlem's degradation, it was as if Baldwin were responding to Hughes's remarks in "Fifth Avenue, Uptown," for *Esquire* magazine in July 1960. He very well could have changed the Fifth to "Filth," since most of his venom was aimed at the projects along that avenue. "The projects in Harlem are hated," he began. "They are hated almost as much as the policemen, and this is saying a great deal. And they are hated for the same reason: both reveal, unbearably, the real attitude of the white world, no matter how many liberal speeches are made, no matter how many lofty editorials are written, no matter how many civil rights commissions are set up."

In effect, they both were right about Harlem, if theater critic and historian Lofton Mitchell is to be the judge. "The small town of black Harlem though surrounded by hostility was crowded with togetherness, love, human warmth, and neighborliness," he discerned. "Southern Negroes fled from physical lynchings and West Indians from economic lynchings. They met in the land north of 110th Street and they brought with them their speech patterns, folkways, mores, and their dogged determination. They brought, too, their religiosity and their gregariousness and they created here a distinct nation that was much like a small town."

Two years earlier, in 1958, Baldwin and Hughes had been seen chatting and posing together with Ralph Ellison at the Newport Jazz Festival. In one of the more than two thousand letters Hughes exchanged with Arna Bontemps, he recalled this meeting, but merely noted that he was there with Ellison and Baldwin. Whatever bonhomie they shared was either disingenuous or soon dissipated a year later with Baldwin's rejection of Hughes's *Selected Poems.* However, either later that year or in the early part of 1959, the enmity between them had begun to thaw. In response to Hughes's request to ship books and art objects to Ghana—the "Gifts for Ghana" campaign—Baldwin sent a few things, though what they were is not known. Hughes acknowledged the gift in a letter to Bontemps in the winter of 1959.

The thaw between the "bard of Harlem" and Baldwin was stopped again in 1962 when they took part in a radio discussion. Hughes insinuated that Baldwin was purposefully currying favor with whites in order to get more speaking engagements. Once more the bitterness between them erupted, and it would intensify when Hughes privately dismissed Baldwin's recently published *Another Country.* After a few critical words about Baldwin's obsession with sex, Hughes declared: "It is a curiously juvenile book for a man who has done so much writing. Neither the style nor the thought is particularly brilliant. Yet it has a certain emotional power. As the characters talk endlessly about their passion and their pain, they reveal a staggering collection of the less commonplace griefs of our time. And this relentless insistence, despite a certain banality and naiveté, ends by conveying an honest and despairing conviction of reality." This sort of damning with faint praise was not at all uncommon for Hughes when it came to Baldwin's works. Each pat on the back seemed to be followed by a stabbing indignation.

Hughes may have fumed even more in the spring of 1963 when he learned of Baldwin's mission to meet with U.S. Attorney General Robert Kennedy, and that he was not among those invited. With Baldwin's *The Fire Next Time,* Hughes was again livid, forwarding an unsolicited essay to the *New York Post* that chastised Baldwin for his poor political judgment about integration and the civil rights movement. Baldwin, he asserted, had offered no solution to the racial crisis then pervading the nation. "The solution he now leaves up to white America," he wrote. "Maybe Baldwin can just cry, 'Fire,' and not have the least idea how to put it out. Or maybe he knows what to do, but will not tell us. Maybe he does not wish to face the next McCarthy."

Above all this screed assailed Baldwin for his increased involvement with the civil rights movement and leaders who had ignored Hughes, a movement he had ignored. One legendary Harlem leader, Anna Arnold Hedgeman, applauded Baldwin's boldness. Baldwin's essay in the *New Yorker* raged with particular poignancy for Hedgeman. His article had caught the attention of white America, she wrote, and "we smiled a bit at these people, because James Baldwin had actually said those things which W.E.B. Du Bois had said with equal beauty and vigor forty years ago. Even as we smiled, we were glad that at last the public media had put into print every word of the beautifully written and true story of the angry, impatient, disgusted and cynical mood of the Negro." Ross Posnock agrees that Baldwin's ideas link him to Du Bois, certainly as they pertain to "internation" and "national unity."

David Leeming, who worked as Baldwin's secretary and assistant from 1963 to 1967, recalled an encounter between Hughes and Baldwin late one night in 1964 at Jenny Lou's, a Harlem restaurant. "After we ordered porgy and grits, the specialty of the house, at the counter, Baldwin suggested that if I look at the man in the corner of the booth nearest the back wall I would be looking at one of the great poets. At about the same moment Hughes saw Baldwin, smiled, and made a wide gesture of invitation with both arms. We joined him at his booth, and a long relaxed conversation followed, first about Jenny Lou's and the welcoming 'Negro ambience' that prevailed there and in Harlem generally, then about race and art. About the latter they disagreed, but the discussion never became rancorous." Their disagreement, Leeming continued, centered on Baldwin's negative treatment of Harlem, which was "home" for Hughes. For Baldwin, he said, Harlem had become nothing more than "a place to collect material for prophecy." In a later reply to Hughes's accusations, Baldwin told his assistant that "Hughes needed to get 'out of Harlem' so that he could look at it."

Neither Baldwin nor Hughes—one accused of exploiting its deprivation and the other charged with romanticizing the squalor—ever applied an economic analysis as pertinent as those in a collection of essays by Dr. John Henrik Clarke. Harlem was not and never had been a self-contained community, Clarke concluded in 1964. "It is owned and controlled by outsiders. "It is a black community with a white economic heartbeat." Only a few of the stores in the community were owned by African Americans, he continued. "A system of pure economic colonialism exists in the Harlem community. This colonialism extends into politics, religion, and every money-making endeavor that touches the life of a Harlem resident." Clarke further noted, taking a page from Hughes's plaint, that Baldwin had accumulated a cult of white followers who flocked to his appearances as if to "some masochistic ceremony of penance." Of course, he added, none of this was Baldwin's doing, nor were those people under his control. In his later years, Clarke would be less fretful about Baldwin's ascendance, and this was particularly true during the heated sixties, when as part of a group of intellectuals targeted by the acerbic Harold Cruse, they were forced into an alliance.

Hughes had his share of white sycophants at his beck and call, too. And there were other commonalities between him and Baldwin, all of which might have been expected traits for two writers of such renown. "The two writers had much more in common than either was willing to admit," wrote W. J. Weatherby about an earlier, more contentious stage of their relationship. Those common elements—for example, mourning the brutal death of Patrice Lumumba, the Congo's first president, or examining the intricacies and realities of negritude—would become more evident as Baldwin matured and Hughes gazed upon the twilight of his career.

As a progenitor of the Harlem Renaissance, Hughes was

in advance of the negritude movement of the 1930s. The key figures of that movement—Aimé Césaire, Léon Damas, Jacques Roumain, Jean Price-Mars, René Maran, and Léopold Senghor—all in their separate ways had paid homage to Hughes and his cohorts for providing the inspiration for the movement, which stressed the importance of identifying with one's African heritage. "I remember very well that around that time we read the poems of Langston Hughes and Claude McKay," Césaire told writer René Depestre. While Césaire said he was not directly influenced by black American artists, "at least I felt that the movement in the United States created an atmosphere that was indispensable for a very clear coming to consciousness." Baldwin's encounters with negritude and a few of its founders would not occur in a meaningful way until September 19, 1956, when he attended and covered the Conference of Negro-African Writers and Artists in the Sorbonne's Amphithéâtre Descartes, in Paris. Among the speakers, most impressive for Baldwin besides Richard Wright were Senghor, later to be the president of Senegal; cultural authority and editor of the *Présence Africaine,* Alioune Diop; anthropologist and linguist Cheikh Anta Diop (not related to Alioune); and Césaire. "Césaire is a caramel-colored man from Martinique, probably around forty, with a great tendency to roundness and smoothness, physically speaking and with the rather vaguely benign air of a school-teacher," Baldwin remembered. "All this changes the moment he begins to speak. It becomes at once apparent that his curious, slow-moving blandness is related to the grace and patience of a jungle cat and that the intelligence behind those spectacles is of a very penetrating and demagogic order." Thus Hughes and Baldwin bracketed the negritude move-

ment, one arriving before the movement was truly underway
and the other witnessing it toward the end of its vibrancy.

At the very beginning of their exchanges, Hughes clearly recognized the insecurities of the fledgling writer, and toward
his last days Baldwin himself realized the anxieties an aging
writer experiences with the arrival of a new breed of artists,
each seeking to dethrone him in the same way he challenged
Richard Wright. LeRoi Jones (Amiri Baraka) was one writer
who over the years had a roller-coaster relationship with
Baldwin. Sometimes they were bitterly opposed, but in the
end they reconciled their differences. (Some of the new rap-
prochement between them may have been generated by
Blues for Mr. Charlie, which hit Broadway to mixed reviews,
though Jones said it was one of the great theater experiences
of his life.)

In November, Josephine Baker, the flamboyant chanteuse
who had fled America in 1925 to become the toast of Paris,
clearly gauged at least the literary differences between Baldwin and Hughes when she sought to combine their talents in
the writing of her life story. As she saw it, Hughes would
write the American part of her odyssey, "the real home side,"
she proposed, and Baldwin would be responsible for her
"revolutionary" aspect. But Hughes had other offers and
passed on the possibility of working with Baldwin. Since
such a pairing was not proposed as a true collaboration, it
might have been less fractious and combustible than Hughes's
debacle with Zora Neale Hurston on *Mule Bone*, which ruptured what warmth and love they had for each other. Nearly
a decade later, in 1973, Baker, through the efforts of Henry
Louis Gates, Jr., would meet with Baldwin, but if her previ-

ous intentions to have Baldwin write a portion of her autobiography were discussed at this time—the last meeting between Baldwin and Baker—it does not occur in Gates's published account.

By the time of Hughes's death in 1967, he and Baldwin were no longer concerned about what the other said or did, though Hughes, a year before his death, had taken a final swipe at Baldwin, lumping him with LeRoi Jones as a purveyor of "primitive, dirty and dangerous" literature. His association of Baldwin with Jones was easy to do. They often appeared in public together and shared the podium at several events, and sometimes read their more recent works, as they would do in 1970 at New York's Town Hall in a fundraising event for Kenneth Gibson, a mayoral candidate in Newark.

Upon hearing of Hughes's passing, Baldwin wrote a note to a friend with enduring accolades for the poet and saying that he would miss his smile, "which always welcomed and always forgave." As in his topsy-turvy relationship with Malcolm X, Baldwin's final words for Hughes bore none of the scorn and acrimony, but remembered only the give and take, the intellectual repartee and jousting that had mutually refined their furious passages.

Chapter 4

Sanctuary

Though Baldwin was raised in the "lap of the church," in a community of saints, it wasn't until he was fourteen, and struggling to adapt to his first year of high school at DeWitt Clinton in the Bronx, that he admits to having a "prolonged religious crisis." "I use the word 'religious,'" he warned, "in the common, and arbitrary sense, meaning that I then discovered God, His saints and angels, and His Hell."

The beginning of puberty is often accompanied by trauma and doubts. One only has to recall the experiences of Richard Wright and Malcolm X when they were fourteen. Each of them was cut adrift from family and challenged to find his way in an unforgiving world. (Emmett Till was also fourteen when he was tragically killed in Mississippi in the summer of 1955. His death haunted Baldwin, who would later use the incident as inspiration for his play *Blues for Mr. Charlie*.) John Grimes, the youthful protagonist of *Go Tell It on the Mountain*, is fourteen when Baldwin begins to relate his tale.

Baldwin was obviously troubled at that age, trying to adjust to a new environment, the demands of his religious background, and his perplexing sexuality. There was also the living terror of the brutal streets of Harlem—something that Wright and Malcolm were not to encounter until they were adults. The church was the chosen sanctuary. "For the wages of sin were visible everywhere," he confessed in *The Fire Next Time*, "in every wine-stained and urine-splashed hallway, in every clanging ambulance bell, in every scar on the faces of pimps and whores . . . in every pistol fight on the Avenue."

Along with the temptations of the "Avenue," which he meant collectively, there were a multitude of dangers that frightened the more fragile residents, and Baldwin navigated the streets alertly with sharp attention to the pitfalls that might find him in the clutches of nasty white policemen who were just as quick to arrest him as to call him a "nigger." In fact, juvenile arrests of African Americans in New York City, principally in Harlem, had soared in 1938 to 25 percent. Moreover, the streets of Harlem were electrified with rallies from protesters led by the Reverend Adam Clayton Powell, Jr. and by black nationalists fueled with the fiery rhetoric of Carlos Cooks. Even the church, where Baldwin fled for refuge, was no hiding place, according to Harlem's more activist ministers. They declared, "We're tired of religion that puts us to sleep. We've got to put religion to work—for us!"

The summer of 1938 had been tumultuous enough in Harlem after Joe Louis knocked out Max Schmeling in the first round of their second fight, to avenge his earlier defeat by the German. The celebrations had an element of turmoil and distress, especially from those unmindful of the law, personal property, safety, and respect for others. The streets of

Harlem, jammed as they were by pedestrians, were always something to be negotiated with care, lest you get sucked into its muck, and soon find it difficult to free yourself from its entrapments, its sinful inducements. There was also a dispute between Councilman Joseph Baldwin, of no relation to the author, and the New York Police Department about the number of homicides over the past year. Councilman Baldwin had claimed there was "a murder-a-day" in Harlem in 1938. This figure was refuted by the police, who put the number of homicides at 82. "It would be impossible for us to fail to report 250 or 300 homicides a year," a police spokesman said. Whatever the count, Baldwin ran to the church, which he knew and where he was welcomed with open arms.

If there was succor in the church, the boy preacher's grades suffered at DeWitt Clinton. That he would encounter problems in high school was to some extent forecast before he arrived there. "I graduated from Douglass in the spring term of 1938," he wrote upon leaving junior high school. "That is to say, I was neither hopelessly bad nor exceptionally good. I crammed for tests . . . as students have done from time immemorial. I did no more work than I thought necessary, played more than I should have, exasperated most of my patient teachers, and in general behaved like a schoolboy." His dalliances would grow once he reached high school, since his literary pursuits increased, including working on the *Magpie*, the school's magazine; there were also sermons to prepare, despite his being plagued by religious uncertainties.

When Baldwin received his first high school report card it was a disaster: he had flunked nearly all of his courses, except English and history, which served to keep his "smart" reputation intact. He had devoted so much time and attention to questioning his faith and the need to succeed in the church–if nothing more than to best his father from the pulpit–that school, except for the *Magpie* and its staff, held no appeal.

It didn't take long before "the boy preacher" outdistanced his father, gaining the kind of celebrity status that pushed schoolwork further and further from his mind. "My youth quickly made me a much bigger drawing card than my father," he wrote. "I pushed this advantage ruthlessly, for it was the most effective means I had found of breaking his hold over me. That was the most frightening time of my life, and quite the most dishonest, and the resulting hysteria lent great passion to my sermons–for a while." No matter the "hysteria," the dishonesty of the experience, he admitted that the church was very exciting. On more than one occasion he would recall the "power and glory" he felt when he and the church were one.

But the rapture he received from those moments were not enough to hold him in the ministry. Literature, particularly the works of Dostoevsky, beckoned him away from the theater of the pulpit. And this renewed passion for reading the great books replaced the biblical stories, the Jewish heroes of the Old Testament who were his consorts and the source of his sermons. He was basically wary of the Bible, offering this comment in 1964: "My own attitude toward the Bible, for instance, is still somewhat ambiguous because the people who brought it to me didn't themselves believe it."

The classic books also made it easier for him to relinquish the church, to set aside his daily encounters with Jewish students who brought Christianity and his color into question. Even more disconcerting, Baldwin began to wonder about his mission, and how he was being used by the church and the pastors to increase the tithes, to bolster the church's building funds; and there was the utter hypocrisy, which came like the slap to his face from his angry father.

By the time he was sixteen, Baldwin no longer needed the sanctuary of the church; his new testament was found in the great books of the Western world, which was a conduit to his own desire for literary expression. To salvage his literary soul it was necessary to abandon the church, to sever ties with a faith that he never seemed to truly accept. In effect, as one writer put it, he left the pulpit in order to preach the gospel. It was a paradox reminiscent of the career change that Aimé Césaire, the great writer from Martinique and a founder of negritude, made in the 1930s. "You could say that I became a poet by renouncing poetry," he said.

Several stories published in the *Magpie* reflect Baldwin's desire to end his relationship with the ministry. The "epitaph to his dissolution" was etched in a short essay, "Incident in London." In the concluding paragraphs of a sketch, Baldwin wrote: "Long before, when the man was young, and before he had gone off to the many wars that were always being fought, he had believed implicitly in the faith he had been taught. He had believed in God, in peace, in righteousness, and the dignity and decency of man. But after he had fought, and had seen how strife degraded and destroyed humanity, his faith had lost its glory and had disappeared." Seeking protection from flying shrapnel, the man hurried to a chapel. "And suddenly the skies blazed fire, and the stars were blotted out, and a roar of fury filled the universe. And slowly the chapel crumbled to the white, still earth. And the street was as it had been before, save that the chapel had been destroyed, and the snow was no longer pure, but filthy, and the man was dead."

This was a prelude to his final sermon. "I remember my last sermon," he said, "I remember it because I knew it was my last. It was a sermon to me. 'Set thy house in order.'"

Setting his house in order meant he had to disobey the order of his pastor to return to the church, a church, according to his brother George, that was right around the corner from where they lived. "Elder Sobers was the minister there," George said. "It was Fireside Church and it was located on 136th Street and Fifth Avenue. This was a storefront church with a relatively small congregation, and Jimmy was highly respected." James's status at the church made it all the more imperative for Elder Sobers to demand his return, though Baldwin by now was convinced that "I didn't believe anymore . . . and didn't believe the lies I was telling."

Later, in several interviews, Baldwin would give conflicting stories about his separation from the church, though some people contend that he never really left the church, but rather merely found another less sacred, more secular pulpit from which to deliver his sermons. No doubt these moments in the church were mined to great success in his first two commercially successful literary endeavors—*Go Tell It on the Mountain* and *The Amen Corner*. David, in *The Amen Corner*, like Baldwin forsakes the church and goes "into the world." Depending on the situation or the interviewer, Baldwin tended to have different memories of events, and whether it was the pull of the film *Native Son*, starring Canada Lee, or a musical by Gilbert and Sullivan, each was just a convenient rationale, a bridge to justify his loss of faith, the adoption of the arts as his salvation. Hadn't he told his stepfather that he would rather write than preach?

The sanctuary of the church was becoming less apparent for the young evangelist by his second year in robes, which meant Baldwin was again vulnerable to the menace of the Harlem streets, a menace that even endangered the most wary street boy, as he considered himself. Believing he was undesirable, Baldwin felt he was not a target for any sort of sexual overtures, but there's a predator, he learned, for even the most nondescript person. "Shortly after I turned sixteen," he recalled in "Here Be Dragons," published two years before his death, "a Harlem racketeer, a man of about thirty-eight, fell in love with me, and I will be grateful to that man until the day I die. I showed him all my poetry, because I had no one else in Harlem to show it to, and even now, I sometimes wonder what on earth his friends could have been thinking, confronted with this stingy-brimmed, musta-chioed, razor-toting Poppa and skinny, pop-eyed Me when he walked me (rarely) into various shady joints, I drinking ginger ale, he drinking brandy." In effect, Baldwin was turned out, and while he loved the man, in "a boy's way," he was nonetheless tormented. And the depth of that torment would be considerable, creeping into his fiction in a very obvious way.

In *Just Above My Head*, Arthur Montana recounts an incident that happened to him when he was thirteen, three years younger than Baldwin was when he experienced a similar encounter. "He was about thirty or forty," Montana told his brother, Hall, "a very rough-looking dude, tall and thin . . ." He told Montana that he was a cute boy and then, "He took out *his* cock, and I just stared at that thing pointing at me, and man, you know how we were raised. I did not know *who* to scream for, and then he put his hand on *my* cock and my cock jumped and then I couldn't move at all. I just stood there, waiting, paralyzed, and he opened my pants and took it out, and it got big and I had never seen it that way, it was the first time and so it meant that I must be just like this man, and then he knelt down and took it in his mouth. I thought he was going to bite it off. But, all the time, it kept getting bigger, and I started to cry." A shorter version of this same incident appears in *Tell Me How Long the Train's Been Gone.* Here he relates that he was picked up by a Harlem racketeer named Johnnie, a big, Spanish-looking guy. He took Leo Proudhammer, the narrator, home "and gave me my first drink of brandy, and took me to bed. He frightened me, or his vehemence, once the lights were out, frightened me, and I didn't like it, but I liked *him*."

In both the fictional and nonfictional version, Montana (Baldwin) was primed for the odyssey out of Harlem and into the world. And this "into the world" would ring like a mantra in *The Amen Corner.* Soon, with his sexuality now strongly aroused, Greenwich Village became his new retreat, not so much as shelter, but as a place where he found comfort in his new pursuits among white girls and homosexuals, something that must not have happened much in Harlem, since Baldwin didn't mention it.

So, Baldwin had found a fresh sanctuary, miles from Harlem and that special hill in Central Park, miles from the church, miles from the literary comfort of the *Magpie,* and deep into the beckoning arms of other men.

Chapter 5

Death in Harlem

One week in the summer of 1943 witnessed the confluence of several notable events in Baldwin's life and Harlem's history. On July 29, Baldwin's stepfather, David, died and on the same day his sister, Paula, was born. A few days later, on August 2, as Baldwin remembered it—though it really happened August 1—while the family was attending David's funeral, on Baldwin's nineteenth birthday, a riot erupted in Harlem.

Baldwin was downtown celebrating his birthday with some friends when the riot broke out. "A Negro soldier, in the lobby of the Braddock Hotel, got into a fight with a white policeman over a Negro girl," Baldwin reported in *Notes of a Native Son*. Angered by the rumor that the black soldier had been shot in the back by the cop and killed while defending the woman, blacks in Harlem took to the streets, looking for a white person to attack and beat in revenge. It made no difference given the pent-up emotions of black Harlemites that the soldier had not been shot, and was not dead—they were poised for a disturbance, an opportunity to vent their hostility and frustration at economic conditions not yet mollified by America's entry into World War II. Harlem's eruption might have also been triggered by the outbreak of riots in other parts of the country, most notably in Mobile, Alabama, and in Detroit, where disgruntled black workers experienced hate strikes or racism from white workers in automobile plants.

"The effect, in Harlem . . . was like the effect of a lit match in a tin of gasoline," Baldwin wrote. "The mob gathered before the doors of the Hotel Braddock [located on Eighth Avenue near 126th Street] simply began to swell and to spread in every direction, and Harlem exploded."

Baldwin observed that the riot did not cross the ghetto lines. Rather than invade the white neighborhoods at Morningside Park or the east side of the Grand Central railroad tracks at 125th Street, the mobs advanced on the vestiges of white power—the stores on 125th Street. Along all the major streets and avenues the army of blacks broke store windows, pried open doors, and randomly looted, running off with anything and everything they could carry. "I truly had not realized that Harlem had so many stores until I saw them all smashed open," Baldwin continued. "The first time the word *wealth* ever entered my mind in relation to Harlem was when I saw it scattered in the streets."

Much of what Baldwin saw and recorded was during the ride to the cemetery to bury his stepfather. Looking at the ruined streets, piles of debris, the shattered glass, and the ravaged stores, he said, "That bleakly memorable morning I hated the unbelievable streets and the Negroes and whites who had, equally, made them that way."

More than six thousand policemen had been summoned

to stop the riot and Governor Thomas Dewey alerted National Guard units. When it was finally quelled, six people, all black, had been killed and 185 injured, and property damage was estimated at $5 million. One Hundred and Twenty-fifth Street was so choked with litter that traffic had to be diverted. While the press had characterized the upheaval as a race riot, Councilman Adam Clayton Powell, Jr. called it an "economic riot." He viewed it as "blind smoldering resentment against Jim Crow of Negro men and women in the Armed forces . . . the increasing rents and failure of the OPA [Office of Price Administration, a federal agency established in 1942 to prevent wartime inflation] to establish rent control . . . the wide flourishing of the black market in Harlem."

Blind was a word that Walter White, then executive secretary of the NAACP, also used to describe the riot. "Blind, unreasoning fury swept the community with the speed of lightning," he wrote. White had been summoned to the disturbance by Mayor Fiorello LaGuardia, who called him requesting that they meet at the West 123rd Street precinct. "LaGuardia," Baldwin recalled, "declared Harlem off-limits except, in effect, for those servicemen who had the right, or no choice but to live there—which was like declaring, in a paroxysm of honesty, that American democracy was an item for export only."

The NAACP leaders were subsequently asked by the mayor to tour the streets to see if they could curb the spreading violence. White's first thought in appealing to the rioters was to assemble such prominent and highly respected musicians and sports figures as Cab Calloway, Duke Ellington, or Joe Louis to speak to them, but all of them were out of town. It was left to the NAACP leaders and Powell and Ferdinand Smith, a member of the Communist Party and president of the National Maritime Union, to explain through bullhorns that the rumors were false about the death of a black soldier.

Twelve hours later the riot was down to a simmer and just about spent. "The riot had profound consequences on black leadership, too" wrote Kenneth Robert Janken in his biography of Walter White. "Mary McLeod Bethune, close friend of Eleanor Roosevelt and a reliably conservative African American voice, compared Harlem's rioters to the participants in the Boston Tea Party; they were simply responding to FDR's call to defend the Four Freedoms and fight international fascism."

Because Baldwin had returned to Harlem to attend his stepfather's funeral he was able to get an immediate, first-hand look at the plunder. For more than a year he had been living in New Jersey, coming back to Harlem only to visit his family, to give them some money, and to go by the hospital to see his ailing stepfather. "I left home—Harlem—in 1942," he said in *No Name in the Street*. He left Harlem, but as I've noted in several places here, Harlem never left him. As he often said, one had to make a voyage far away in order to come full circle. But it would take years before he fully understood the essence of this paradox; otherwise he was wrought with guilt, seeking all sorts of ways to justify leaving his family. "I left in Harlem a family and a faith, and this is never done without terrible misgivings," he said in a letter to friend Dan Fink, who was serving in the military. The letter was written on St. Valentine's Day in 1943. "And what I ran to was, I very soon realized, not enough.

My novel was to be, in a sense, my justification. The implement of my defiance, and the wedge that would open the door on the life I wanted." Thirty years later, these feelings about Harlem were unaltered: "There is a sense in which I could say I never have left Harlem. But there is another sense in which I certainly never can go back there, if only because [the] Harlem in which I was born exists no longer. And though that rupture has something to do with race, it also has something to do with a nature or quality or the specialness—I don't know what the word is—of human experience."

Elements of the community were often profoundly interwoven in his novels, essays, articles, short stories, and speeches. Like the sundry other paradoxes that gripped him, Baldwin's love and disdain for his native Harlem was pressured into dissimilar forms. Even when he left home to work in New Jersey in defense plants, there were always issues summoning him home, and when he returned in June 1943, a few weeks before pandemonium broke loose in Harlem, it was to deal with his stepfather's health and his mother's confinement. In fact, he returned to Harlem out of breath, having fled from a restaurant in Trenton where he had hurled a water mug in outrage at a waitress after being told, "We don't serve Negroes."

It was a rage that Baldwin rarely expressed physically. That kind of disgust he instead alleviated through his writings. Meanwhile, the Harlem he discovered that summer was a simmering cauldron, just waiting to explode, which it did to great loss in lives and property.

With the family's breadwinner dead and his mother burdened with yet another child, Baldwin moved back to

Harlem. His ability to handle a rambunctious bunch of children was desperately needed, and he didn't hesitate, taking a series of menial jobs to pay the rent and to provide food for the family. The only relief he had from a crowded, overbearing Harlem, as he termed it, and the unrelenting noise of children were trips to Greenwich Village and conversations with artist and mentor Beauford Delaney. Delaney finally convinced him to move out of Harlem, if no more than for his peace of mind and to rekindle his creativity, his writing. He moved in with Delaney, though on many nights he found comfort and relief just roaming Times Square. In the early prose of *Another Country* this tedium and boredom are graphically recalled.

"When James did go home, the guilt turned to anger," Ted Gottfried believed. "He was sarcastic to his mother. He treated his sisters badly. He yelled at his brothers. His love for his family was turning to resentment and hate." This is not what George Baldwin remembers. "James helped the best way he could," he said. "When he wasn't changing a diaper or washing the dishes, he was at work, making sure we got something to eat." The children might have made it unbearable at times, but, according to George, his brother was patient. "He had a way of dealing with us and finding time for his writing, too."

Although Baldwin had moved to the Village, his sense of family and their need to have him necessitated weekly trips to Harlem. Soon a pattern was established, one that would characterize his contact with the community for the rest of his life. Visits to Harlem became rarer and only on special occasions would he go physically to the neighborhoods that had nurtured him. Still, Harlem was part of his DNA, inextricably a part of his creative works, where it was treated and characterized with different strokes, depending on the situation. "Though he split from Harlem, I think he still found it necessary to maintain some sort of connection to the community, if even from a transitional venue," said Quincy Troupe. "That's why I think Mikell's bar was chosen, plus his brother, David, was a bartender there. Mikell's, which was located on Columbus at 97th Street, may have been like a DMZ location, not exactly in Harlem, but close enough for him to rendezvous with his friends from both sides of this presumed borderline. And then there was the music at the club, and Jimmy loved his jazz as much as he loved his scotch, particularly Johnnie Walker Black Label."

Meanwhile, Harlem, as he knew so well, would continue to exist, whether he was there or not. Politics in Harlem clearly was doing all right after Baldwin's departure, and was nowhere more productive than in J. Raymond Jones's George Washington Carver Democratic Club or the Communist Party, which celebrated Benjamin Davis's council victory in 1944. Within a year, Harlemites were even more celebratory as World War II came to an end. Uptown black workers were also in a good mood as *New York Amsterdam News* columnist Earl Brown cheered the local unions and their African American leaders. "In my opinion, the Negro leaders in trade unions are the most genuine in Harlem," he wrote. Brown added that union leaders were more influential than the preachers. Baldwin would not have contested this conclusion, since the inefficacy of black preachers was partly to blame for his rejection of the church.

But irrepressible Harlem and the church ganged up on Baldwin again in 1946. Through his longtime friend and former schoolmate at DeWitt Clinton High School, photographer Richard Avedon, Baldwin met another photographer, Theodore Pelatowski. The relationship was platonic, though Baldwin would have had it otherwise, and together they planned a project to photograph the storefront churches of Harlem, with Baldwin supplying the text. Baldwin's intentions, according to his biographer David Leeming, was one part revelation and one part vengeance as he sought to show "the horrendous dishonesty of the country itself."

They took the assignment with enthusiasm, but the project, like Baldwin's dream of a more carnal affair, was never completed. However, Baldwin's writing in the proposal was so impressive that he was awarded a Rosenwald Fellowship, and later he would use some of the funds to purchase a one-way ticket to France. "When Jimmy decided to leave home," recalled his brother George, "I said to him, 'So, you're getting ready to leave the plantation, huh?' I told him to do me one favor: Tell the truth about this country, if you do nothing else."

Baldwin's first significant essay was published in *Commentary* in February 1948, a few months before he booked passage to Paris. He had been commissioned to write about Harlem and the results caught the attention and jangled the nerves of several individuals, including conservative writer George Schuyler, whom Baldwin dismissed; the owners of the *New York Amsterdam News*; and, most disturbingly, the Jewish community, who felt that Baldwin's comments amounted to anti-Semitism.

Given the accumulating enemies, debts, and only minor literary accomplishments—his short story "Previous Condition" appeared in the October issue of *Commentary* and his essay "Journey to Atlanta," based on the travels of his brother, David, was published in the October edition of *The New Leader*—it was time to get out. A month later, November 11, Armistice Day, Baldwin sailed for France with Harlem still on his mind, his stepfather's death blending with the memory of a community in ruins.

Chapter 6

MALCOLM X

Like Baldwin, Malcolm X (El Hajj Malik El-Shabazz) had a sacred claim on Harlem, though Malcolm was not born there but rather arrived in the early 1940s as a teenager, and would be in and out of the community until his incarceration in 1946. "I first met Malcolm Little in the summer of 1943 up here on Sugar Hill in Harlem," recalled Clarence Atkins. "He was working for the New York Central railroad then, and living not far from me on 147th Street." Atkins said Malcolm would often disappear for days at a time, presumably spending time on the other "Hill" in Roxbury, Massachusetts, where his half sister Ella Collins lived. "We spent many a night drinking and talking at the La Marr-Cherie, which was located at the corner of 146th Street and St. Nicholas."

Atkins said that in Spike Lee's biopic the club's name was changed to the Onyx. For years the La Marr-Cherie building has been abandoned, after a brief life as the Club 721, named for its address on St. Nicholas. Neither Malcolm nor Baldwin would recognize the place today, although hordes of young men congregate there each day to play dominoes and sell drugs, despite the strong odor of urine. It was recently the site for the film *I Now Pronounce You Chuck and Larry*, about an affair between two "gay" firemen and starring Adam Sandler.

When Atkins and Malcolm weren't hobnobbing at the club, they might be found some evenings at Jimmy's Chicken Shack, farther up St. Nicholas Avenue, where Malcolm would later work occasionally, washing dishes with Redd Foxx. While these two future luminaries were scrubbing pots and pans, a few doors from them down the street on St. Nicholas, in a basement apartment, Ralph Ellison was toiling over his masterpiece, *Invisible Man*.

Atkins, a highly respected jazz authority who died in 2004, said Malcolm knew the streets as well as any native, particularly those spots where the hustlers, gamblers, pimps, whores, numbers men, and playboys hung out. He shared an affinity for the streets with Baldwin, a point confirmed by two of Baldwin's most astute biographers, W. J. Weatherby and David Leeming. Baldwin told Weatherby that "when he compared their lives, especially their boyhoods in the streets, he identified with Malcolm more than with any of the other black leaders." In what could have been the first meeting between Baldwin and Malcolm, the two men appeared in Chicago on April 25, 1961, to discuss integration on a radio program moderated by Princeton Professor Eric Goldman. They apparently got along reasonably well because Baldwin subsequently met with the Nation of Islam's leader, Elijah Muhammad, perhaps at Malcolm's suggestion, Leeming noted. This first encounter was a prelude to their famous debate two years later.

Without specifying exactly where or when, Baldwin said,

I saw Malcolm before I met him. I had just returned from someplace like Savannah, I was giving a lecture somewhere in New York, and Malcolm was sitting in the first or second row of the hall, bending forward at such an angle that his long arms nearly caressed the ankles of his long legs, staring up at me. I very nearly panicked. I knew Malcolm only by legend, and this legend, since I was a Harlem street boy, I was sufficiently astute to distrust. I distrusted the legend because we, in Harlem, have been betrayed so often.

Moreover, Baldwin said he had heard a great deal about Malcolm, who by this time was the leader of Temple Number Seven, "and I was afraid of him, as was everyone else, and I was further handicapped by having been out of the country for so long."

For Baldwin to have immediately recognized Minister Malcolm in the audience, it must have been after Baldwin's second tour of the South in 1960. (In 1948, Baldwin wrote an essay, "Journey to Atlanta," but he didn't make the trip. Two of his brothers did and it was from them that he got the details.) In the above passage, he may have mistaken Savannah for Charlotte or Atlanta. His first trip had occurred three years earlier, before Malcolm gained national notoriety from *The Mike Wallace Show*, which featured a televised documentary "The Hate That Hate Produced." And though Baldwin was a "Harlem street boy," there is little chance he could have known of Malcolm's reputation from his distant home in France. Even some of the most peripatetic Harlemites had only become aware of Malcolm after the Johnson Hinton incident in the spring of 1957. Upon hearing that Hinton had been severely beaten by the police, Malcolm led a phalanx of Muslims first to the precinct and then to Harlem Hospital, where they refused to move until they were fully assured that their fellow Muslim was out of danger and receiving medical attention. Convinced that things were all right, Malcolm gave a command and his followers dispersed. It was an expression of power that left even the police in awe, and this was just the early sign of charisma that would emanate well beyond the 28th Precinct.

Baldwin may have seen Malcolm in the flesh much earlier, given his own proclivity to prowl the streets of Harlem. "I sometimes found myself in Harlem on Saturday nights, and I stood in the crowds, at 125th Street and Seventh Avenue, and listened to the Muslim speakers," he wrote in *The Fire Next Time*. For at least a generation, soapbox orators had turned this intersection into a veritable Hyde Park, and no speaker commanded audiences as large as Malcolm X, so while Baldwin doesn't mention his name, in all likelihood he heard Malcolm long before they faced off behind microphones or in front of cameras. And he certainly could have been talking about Malcolm in the spring of 1961 when he wrote this about a Muslim speaker: "It is quite impossible to argue with a Muslim concerning the actual state of Negroes in this country—the truth, after all, is the truth. This is the great power a Muslim speaker has over his audience. His audience has not heard this truth—the truth about their daily lives—honored by anyone else."

By 1965, the year of Malcolm's assassination, the "pulpit on the corner" was rarely in use. Had it lasted a few more years there would have been more opportunities for the two men of prominence to meet. This historic meeting spot was slated for demolition by 1969, much to the dismay of local activists, who did all they could to stave off the inevitable. But in the end the street orators had to find another place to "speak to the people," and Lewis Michaux had to find another location for his National African Memorial Bookstore, popularly known as "The House of Common Sense and Home of Proper Propaganda." It had provided a backdrop for Malcolm and others on many occasions. Soon the clamor was drowned out by noise from the construction of the State Office Building on 125th Street, now named in honor of the legendary minister and Harlem's first black congressman, Adam Clayton Powell, Jr.

Arguably, there was much common sense and proper propaganda exchanged by Baldwin and Malcolm during their debates and discussions. Though wary and somewhat intimidated by Malcolm, Baldwin nonetheless expressed a guarded admiration for the fiery Muslim. "When Malcolm X, who is considered the movement's second-in-command, and heir apparent, points out that the cry of 'violence' was not raised, for example, when the Israelis fought to regain Israel, and, indeed, is raised only when black men indicate that they will fight for their rights, he is speaking the truth," he said. This comment from *The Fire Next Time*, published in 1963, came after Baldwin's debates with Malcolm in 1961 and 1962, and a televised interview he conducted with Malcolm in May 1963, according to a citation in *Malcolm X: The FBI File*, compiled by Clayborne Carson. Those exchanges were no less even-handed and constrained. Malcolm seemed equally diplomatic about Baldwin, reserving his caustic remarks for Dr. King and other civil rights leaders. "When James Baldwin came in from Paris," Malcolm said, referring to Baldwin's scheduled appearance at the historic March on Washington—or "Farce on Washington," as he defined it—"they wouldn't let him talk because they couldn't make him go by the script. Burt Lancaster read the speech that Baldwin was supposed to make." Malcolm made this same point in his famous "Message to the Grass Roots," delivered in Detroit at the King Solomon Baptist Church in late 1963: "They wouldn't let Baldwin get up there because they know Baldwin is liable to say anything."

Evidence of Baldwin's dismay at this situation can be found on page xix of the introduction he wrote to Michael Thelwell's *Duties, Pleasures, and Conflicts: Essays in Struggle*, in 1987. "The official and semi-official opposition to *any* kind of March on Washington was terrified and profound," he lamented. "I had absolutely nothing to do with the March as it evolved, but I was asked to do whatever I could do to prevent it. In my view, by that time, there was, on the one hand, nothing to prevent—the March had already been co-opted—and, on the other, no way of stopping the people from descending on Washington. What struck me most horribly was that virtually no one in power (including some blacks or Negroes who were somewhere next door to power) was able, even remotely, to accept the depth, the dimension, of the passion and the faith of the people."

In a television interview on Gil Noble's *Like It Is* in September 1977, Baldwin said he conceded in order to avoid another rift similar to the one that had surrounded John Lewis's speech, which had to be rewritten with all the "militant rhetoric" extracted. Lewis, with the help of Courtland Cox and James Forman, emended his speech twice to satisfy A. Philip Randolph, the doyen of the march. "The speech still had fire," Lewis recalled in his autobiography. "It still had bite, certainly more teeth than any other speech that day," perhaps including those delivered by Baldwin's proxy.

Several months before the March on Washington, Dr. Kenneth Clark interviewed both Baldwin and Malcolm on separate occasions. When Clark asked Baldwin to elaborate on Malcolm's ability to reach students during his speeches, he said, "What Malcolm tells them in effect, is that they should be proud being black, and God knows that they should be. That is a very important thing to hear in a country which assures you that you should be ashamed of it. Of course, in order to do this, what he does is destroy a truth and invent a history. What he does is say 'you're better because you're black.' Well, of course that isn't true. That's the trouble." Moreover, Baldwin continued, praising Malcolm's ability to speak truth to power and to articulate the suffering and frustration of Black Americans, "That's Malcolm's great authority over any of his audiences. He corroborates their reality; he tells them that they really exist."

These attributes, of course, were also part of Baldwin's arsenal, and Malcolm was probably making reference to them in his comment that Baldwin was muzzled at the March on Washington. Still, Malcolm often relegated Baldwin to the nonviolent camp, deeming his political outlook nothing more than "pseudo-revolt," a comment he made while traveling abroad in 1964. (Malcolm was in Egypt at this time, on a tour of Africa that began July 9 and ended November 24. He was in Egypt on July 18 and met with Muslim educators in Cairo. On August 4 he was in Alexandria to address eight-hundred Muslim students from Africa and Asia. He attended the Second African Summit on August 21.)

When Clark interviewed Malcolm shortly after his session with Baldwin, the Muslim minister saved his mention of Baldwin until his closing response, chastising Baldwin for taking "Negroes" who "pose as leaders, all of whom are married either to white men or white women," to meet with Attorney General Robert F. Kennedy on May 24, 1963, in Joseph Kennedy's apartment at 24 Central Park South. It lasted almost three hours. When you do this, he asserted, "You'll always have a race problem." "When Baldwin took that crew with him to see Kennedy, he took the wrong crew. And as long as they take the wrong crew to talk to that man, you're not going to get anywhere near any solution to this problem in this country." The "crew" Malcolm was referring to included Lena Horne, Harry Belafonte, and Lorraine Hansberry, and Dr. King's attorney, Clarence Jones. Clark was also in that contingent, but with a black wife, he obviously was exempt from Malcolm's stinging indictment. (Clark's interview with Baldwin would occur later that same day, during a taping for a television show on WNDT. The program was produced by Henry Morgenthau, III of WGBH-TV in Boston, who was also at the Kennedy meeting. Also, Malcolm would have been even more incensed to know, if he didn't already, that Baldwin had invited June Shagaloff, an NAACP official and expert on school integration. She didn't attend in an official capacity since none of the leaders of the various civil rights organizations was invited.)

Not even a year after the meeting, Baldwin clearly was not satisfied with Robert Kennedy's half-stepping on the issues. In an interview with a reporter from *Der Spiegel*, a West German newsmagazine, Baldwin warned that an impending racial crisis might explode into a race war, if something wasn't done immediately by the attorney general's office to alleviate the mounting pressure. He accused the FBI of collusion with southern sheriffs and, at the same time, dismissed Kennedy's record on civil rights. Baldwin asserted that blacks in Harlem had been hoarding "weapons for years and for only one purpose: that's the day of unavoidable bloody conflict." The prophet predicted the coming of "absolute social and moral chaos."

Baldwin later admitted that he was a bit surprised at Kennedy's naïveté, and Kennedy expressed his misgivings at how poorly informed his visitors were. And according to FBI reports, Kennedy was even more dismissive, citing Baldwin as a "nut." "They don't know anything," he later told the historian Arthur Schlesinger, Jr. "They don't know what the laws are—they don't know what the facts are—they don't know what we've been doing or what we're trying to do. . . . It was all emotion, hysteria." In *A Thousand Days: John F. Kennedy in the White House*, Schlesinger elaborated on this meeting, adding comments from Clark, who he thought was far more thoughtful than Baldwin when the latter took exception to Kennedy's notion that everybody in the room was blessed. "You don't know what the hell you're talking about," Baldwin snapped. "My life is not blessed. I live in hell." "The fact that Bobby Kennedy sat through such an ordeal for three hours proves he is among the best the white power structure has to offer," Clark said. "There were no villains in that room—only the past of our society."

Malcolm might have sympathized more with Baldwin if he had known the content of the heated exchanges during that meeting, and probably would have applauded Baldwin's retort to Kennedy's notion of the limitations of black Americans and when they might be able to become president of the United States. "I resent that," Baldwin blasted. "What right does the son of a first generation Irish immigrant have to tell me when I can be president? I've been here for 400 years." (In *Ed Brooke: Biography of a Senator*, John Henry Cutler states that Robert Kennedy in fact was a third-generation Irish American, his great-grandfather having arrived in America in 1849.)

This meeting, or altercation, prompted Kennedy to alert FBI Director J. Edgar Hoover and the agency's surveillance of Baldwin, which had begun earlier for reasons indicated below, was intensified. The attorney general went from rage to outrage, according to biographer Evan Thomas, who quotes then deputy attorney general Nicholas Katzenbach as saying, "After Baldwin, he was absolutely shocked. Bobby expected to be an honorary black. It really hurt his feelings, and it was pretty mean. But the fact that he thought he knew so much—and learned he didn't—was important." Baldwin had already been caught in the crosshairs of the FBI as early as 1960, through his association with the Fair Play for Cuba Committee. In 1963, just a few months before the meeting with Kennedy, Baldwin was among a list of signers, also including Carl Braden, who demanded that the Anti-Defamation League withdraw an award given to President John F. Kennedy unless the Department of Justice ceased harassing journalist William Worthy, Jr., who had traveled without a permit to China and Cuba. Less than a week after the meeting with Kennedy, Baldwin spoke at a rally sponsored by CORE (Congress of Racial Equality) at Wagner College on Staten Island. An FBI "Airtel" communication noted that folk singer Leon Bibb opened the show and Baldwin addressed the issue of integration in the South. During the question-and-answer period, Baldwin was asked about his meeting with Kennedy, and his only response was that the attorney general had begun "to listen."

For the most part Baldwin and Malcolm agreed on the issue of integration–as they shared a dislike for the middle class elite–during their debate in 1963, but Baldwin departed radically from Malcolm when he declared that he was not a religious person. "All theologies for me are suspect," Baldwin said, and thus he concluded that Malcolm's theology was just as good (or as bad) as any other. "What I would like to see is a world in which religions are not necessary." Baldwin had clearly moved a considerable distance from those days when he was a teenager preaching the Gospel. Rather than tackle Baldwin's atheist stance, Malcolm found a point of departure on the question of identity, stating that he was "proud to be a black man." Baldwin had no retort to this, perhaps taking his blackness as a given, though he would later take a swipe at Malcolm's name in a poem that wasn't published until the early eighties:

> *Well. Niggers don't own nothing,*
> *got no flag, even our names*
> *are hand-me-downs*
> *and you don't change that*
> *by calling yourself X:*
> *sometimes that just makes it worse,*
> *like obliterating the path that leads back*
> *to whence you came, and*
> *to where you can begin.*

Nevertheless, Malcolm and Baldwin would once again find common ground in their distrust of white liberals, a subject that recurs throughout Baldwin's fiction and nonfiction. In several interviews, Baldwin cited remarks by Malcolm on white liberals. Baldwin told John Hall in the early seventies, "I do believe that what black people have to do, and are doing, is what Malcolm X said we should do. He said to some white liberal: 'You educate your Community, and I'll educate mine. By seeming to work separately, we'll really be working together.'" Baldwin may have lifted this phrase from the last pages of Malcolm's autobiography.

On September 15, 1963, four black girls were killed in a church bombing in Birmingham, Alabama. Baldwin spoke in New York City, and his passionate words rang with all the intensity of a Malcolm speech. His pain was obvious as he practically denounced the philosophy of nonviolence, in the same way he had renounced Christianity, giving him another commonality with Malcolm. This emotional charge would color his speeches more and more as the civil rights movement gathered momentum, heading inexorably toward the assassination of Malcolm X in February 1965 and the Selma march a few weeks later.

In the mid-sixties, Baldwin's ideas, like Dr. King's, were beginning to dovetail with Malcolm's. Baldwin rarely gave an interview after Malcolm's death that didn't include a quote or two from Malcolm. "White is a state of mind" was one of his favorites. "Malcolm, finally," Baldwin wrote in *No Name in the Street*, "was a genuine revolutionary, a virile impulse long since fled from the American way of life—in himself, indeed, he was a kind of revolution, both in the sense of a return to a former principle, and in the sense of an

upheaval. It is pointless to speculate on his probable fate had
he been legally white. Given the white man's options, it is
probably just as well for all of us that he was legally black. In
some church someday, so far unimagined and unimaginable,
he will be hailed as a saint."

On January 12, 1961, Baldwin spoke at a rent strike rally in
a gym on 117th Street. It had been called by the Rent Coordinating Committee, which must have included the fiery Jesse
Gray among its speakers. More than 800 people attended. "It
isn't only the landlord you have to fight, it is also the insurance
companies," Baldwin told a receptive audience. "In spite of all
the policemen walking in Harlem my brother has been robbed
four times in the last six months. And nothing is done about it.
One doesn't even call the police anymore. It isn't worth it.
This is what we are trying to fight against." Once again, Baldwin found the time and energy to lend his powerful voice to
an important cause in Harlem.

However, he was reluctant to condone a civil rights protest at the New York World's Fair in 1964–65. Led by the
Brooklyn CORE (Congress of Racial Equality), many of the
protesters participating in the stall-in–blocking the entry to
the New York State Pavilion–were forcibly removed by fair
security. "Well, my reaction, my view was not to stall-in on
the way to the World's Fair," he told radio commentator
Barry Gray on WMCA on May Day. "Let the world in
because we needed the world to witness, let them in. Challenge it while the world is there . . . We don't need a stall-in
for the very practical reason that the country is already so
congested nobody can get anywhere anyway." Baldwin's
position and his reasoning anticipated the teach-in strategy a
few years later by activists opposing the war in Vietnam, par-

ticularly those who chose to open the universities to dialogue rather than shutting down the classrooms.

Baldwin and Malcolm may not have been in agreement on most things early in their relationship, but in the days before Malcolm was killed, Baldwin had gained a newfound respect for him, and began to articulate what he believed to be Malcolm's impact on America. And some believed he may have helped Malcolm draft his UN petition to charge the United States with genocide. "This is the first time in the history of this country where people are forced to recognize some facts of Negro life," Baldwin said, speaking of white people's reaction to Malcolm. "It's no longer possible for them to contain it and pretend it isn't true. A man like Malcolm has this utility, that he frightens people so much that finally they'd rather talk even to me than to him."

Baldwin's most extensive discussion of Malcolm—particularly his style of debate—occurs in his collection of essays *No Name in the Street*, published seven years after Malcolm's assassination. Baldwin recounts when he and Malcolm, along with historian C. Eric Lincoln, noted black conservative George Schuyler, and others, took part in a televised panel discussion:

> "Nothing could have been more familiar to me than Malcolm's style in debate. I had heard it all my life. It was vehemently non-stop and Malcolm was young and looked younger; this caused his opponents to suppose that Malcolm was reckless. Nothing could have been less reckless, more calculated, and even to those loopholes he so often left dangling. They were not loopholes at all, but hangman's knots, as whoever rushed for the

loophole immediately discovered. Whenever this happened, the strangling interlocutor invariably looked to me, as being the more "reasonable," to say something which would loosen the knot. Mr. Schuyler often *did* say something, but it was always the wrong thing, giving Malcolm yet another opportunity. All I could do was elaborate on some of Malcolm's points, or modify, or emphasize, or seem to try to clarify, but there was no way I could disagree with him.

Besides debates, there were other occasions when Baldwin and Malcolm were together, especially after Malcolm's tours of Africa and months before his death. For example, Baldwin recalled being with Malcolm and his new baby, who must have been Ilyasah. She was born July 22, 1962, and Malcolm had made his pilgrimage to Mecca in April 1964, after his split with the Nation of Islam. Baldwin asked Malcolm, "'Are you trying to tell me if that child were white you would dash it to the floor because it's a devil's child?' Well, it was a difficult question and he couldn't answer it. Then he went to Mecca and when he returned I knew I didn't need to ask him that question anymore. It was then that American society began regarding him as dangerous." In his essay "To Be Baptized," Baldwin explained further what he meant by the danger Malcolm presented: "What made him unfamiliar and dangerous was not his hatred for white people but his love for blacks, his apprehension of the horror of the black condition, and the reasons for it, and his determination so to work on their hearts and minds that they would be enabled to see their condition and change it themselves." Apparently Malcolm also represented a certain kind of danger to some black Americans. When his life was extinguished in a fusillade of bullets at the Audubon Ballroom in Washington Heights, New York City, on February 21, 1965, Baldwin was in London. "The British press said that I accused innocent people of this murder," Baldwin later explained. "What I tried to say then, and will try to repeat now, is that whatever hand pulled the trigger did not buy the bullet. That bullet was forged in the crucible of the West, that death was dictated by the most successful conspiracy in the history of the world, and its name is white supremacy."

Malcolm was murdered before he and Alex Haley had completed his autobiography, and upon its publication the *New York Times* contacted Baldwin to review it. But Baldwin's hectic schedule, to say nothing of his notorious inability to meet deadlines, made it virtually impossible for him to fulfill this assignment. Baldwin, as several close associates noted, was evidently not ready to deal with Malcolm, at least not until he could handle him on his own terms. That opportunity would have to wait, since he was in the midst of dealing with the circumstances surrounding the Harlem Six, and with a number of other speaking engagements, including a return to Harlem to speak at Frederick Douglass Junior High School, an all-boy institution and his alma mater. He had spoken at the school in 1963 when he told a student body of some five-hundred members that "color is not important. Color doesn't matter. Color is a political reality which certain politicians use. There is no moral value to black or white skin." On this return he was there to honor an "alumnus of the year" award. It was also possibly to fulfill a promise to his nephew, James, then a student at the school.

Toward the fall of 1963, Baldwin was not too busy to write a letter in support of *Liberation* magazine (not to be confused with the *Liberator*). This letter, composed October 3, was basically a plea for funds, and Baldwin was lending his good name to induce people to subscribe. The magazine had been founded in 1956 by a number of antiwar radicals and pacifists, including A. J. Muste, Bayard Rustin, and David Dellinger. "As a writer, I am deeply convinced that the world of the pen is essential if we are to intensify and motivate the work of the mass movement," Baldwin averred. "There is no revolution without theory. Moreover, in the flood-tide of the struggle for racial justice, as in the struggle for peace, not only is a philosophy required, but an ever renewed radicalization, a striving to go to the roots of our social problems and to solve them. For this *Liberation* is uniquely indispensable." The missive may have been partly inspired by the March on Washington, which energized Baldwin and a corps of other activists. It showed again how tireless Baldwin was and the extent to which he put aside his literary pursuits to attend to what he saw as vital political matters.

After resisting several overtures from Hollywood moguls and matinee idols to write screenplays, Baldwin accepted an offer from Columbia to develop a script on the life of Malcolm X. In August 1967 he began conferring with director Elia Kazan, of *On the Waterfront* fame, and Alex Haley, the coauthor of Malcolm's autobiography. That he was able to even draft a treatment is amazing, given all the distractions he faced, and none were more consuming on the West Coast than his association with the Black Panther Party. Meetings, parties, rallies, and fund-raisers for and with the Panthers kept him from his appointed task, and this mission was further encumbered with the arrival of Dr. King and members of the Southern Christian Leadership Conference. Even more daunting were the guidelines from the studio placing restrictions on his artistic vision. He was told to avoid any discussion of Malcolm in Mecca, and Baldwin soon understood that what they wanted was a sanitized version of Malcolm's life. He might have been further upset by a rumor that Charlton Heston might be asked to portray Malcolm in blackface. Billy Dee Williams was Baldwin's choice for the role. Baldwin expressed delight at the prospect in a letter to his brother David. Baldwin had just seen a film Williams was in, *Slow Dance on the Killing Floor*, and was very impressed with his performance and how he looked. "He's beautiful. Period," Baldwin gushed. "I've found my Malcolm." However, Baldwin's timetable was further disrupted when he learned that Dr. King had been assassinated. He was devastated. First it was his friend Medgar Evers, the NAACP stalwart killed by Klan members in June 1963, then Malcolm, and now Martin was gone. All of them, he concluded, were noble men. There was not enough liquor, not enough scotch whiskey to wash away his sorrow.

In 1968, a year before beginning work on the screenplay, Baldwin participated in a memorial service for Malcolm at I.S. (Intermediate School) 201 in Harlem, located at 127th Street and Madison, and he was returning again to the vicinity where he lived as a child. According to FBI reports, the auditorium was full to capacity, with approximately seven hundred people in attendance. Among the speakers at the event were Conrad Lynn, LeRoi Jones, Betty Shabazz, and activist/school principal Herman Ferguson, an aide to Malcolm who was subsequently hounded out of the country for his radical politics. Other than his laudatory remarks about Malcolm, the FBI did not provide a full account of Baldwin's speech.

Adding to the sad turn of events, his screenplay was rejected and he reluctantly accepted the veteran "script doctor" Arnold Perl to assist him on technical matters. The partnership with Perl, however, could not salvage the project, and Baldwin felt it was time to end it. "To make a long story short," he told Jewell Handy Gresham in a 1976 interview, "I walked out with my script. To put it brutally, if I had agreed with Hollywood, I would have been allowing myself to create an image of Malcolm that would have satisfied them and infuriated you, broken your hearts. At one point I saw a memo that said, among other things, that the author had to avoid giving any political implications to Malcolm's trip to Mecca. Now, how can you write about Malcolm X without writing about his trip to Mecca and its political implications? It was not surprising. They were doing the Che Guevara movie while I was out there. It had nothing to do with Latin America, the United Fruit Company, Che Guevara, Cuba . . . nothing to do with anything. It was hopeless crap. Hollywood's fantasy is designed to prove to you that this poor, doomed nitwit deserves his fate." Baldwin said he would not take part in "a second assassination" of Malcolm X.

That screenplay was later published in 1972 as a "scenario" based on Malcolm's life, titled *One Day, When I Was Lost*. Baldwin, refusing to compromise his principles or Malcolm's, provides a moving account of Malcolm's travails to get into Mecca, much of which is word for word from the autobiography. Nowhere is Elijah Muhammad's name mentioned, though there is a character that roughly approximates him and his often turbulent relationship with Malcolm. Conveniently, too, the Nation of Islam is called the Movement, and there are other ways in which Baldwin sidestepped possible libel or slander. To what degree Perl helped Baldwin in the adaptation of the screenplay is questionable since it was by no means done in a conventional format. But Baldwin's efforts were not entirely dispatched to the dustbin; there was a documentary based on the script that very few people, including Baldwin, ever saw. And the script to some extent influenced Spike Lee when he finally brought his biopic to the nation's screens. Lee, according to Ralph Wiley, who later collaborated with Lee on a book about the making of the film, liked the first third of Baldwin's script, but he "didn't know how to handle Elijah Muhammad." Moreover, Lee contended, "Baldwin had stuff out of order. He had Malcolm giving speeches at the beginning of the movie that didn't really come until 1963 or 1964, so we had to get rid of those." Lee would have been better served if he had retained those segments of Baldwin's script where Malcolm is seen in consultation with Africans during his tour of the continent. That notwithstanding, neither Baldwin nor Lee offered any extensive review of Malcolm's last, most productive year as an ambassador from black America, and as a world statesman.

Baldwin was dead by the time Lee's film was completed, and perhaps his final comment on the whole affair can be summed up in the words he placed in Betty Shabazz's mouth at the end of his script, as she mourns the loss of her husband: "You are present when you are away." Malcolm had been dead for about seven years when Baldwin put the script aside, but there is little doubt that Malcolm retained a powerful presence in Baldwin's memory, "his extraordinary gentleness." Malcolm mentioned Baldwin's name only once in his autobiography and that was to note his literary impact.

Earlier he had told Baldwin that if he was the "warrior of the revolution," then Baldwin "was the poet." In many ways, the roles could have been reversed.

For all the philosophical distance between Baldwin and Malcolm–and that distance was considerably smaller with each passing day of their lives–they can never know how close they are through eternity: their names are inscribed, along with those of Langston Hughes and Paul Robeson, in the Walk of Fame on 135th Street near Frederick Douglass Boulevard, and they rest in peace several yards from each other at the Ferncliff Cemetery in Hartsdale, Westchester County, New York.

Chapter 7

THE HARLEM SIX

On April 17, 1964, in Harlem . . . a young man, father of two, left a customer's apartment and went into the streets. There was a great commotion in the street, which, especially since it was a spring day, involved many people, including running, frightened, little boys. They were running from the police." Thus opens Baldwin's essay "A Report from Occupied Territory." The words also marked the beginning of his involvement in an incident that would attract (and distract) him for the next four years, and much longer for a coterie of other activists.

Baldwin didn't publish this article until two years after the turmoil had settled into the community's collective memory. Ultimately, the tragedy would be labeled "The Harlem Six," which despite its significance for local residents failed to grab national headlines like the Trenton Six (who faced the electric chair on murder convictions but were later freed) and the Martinsville Seven (all seven were executed, convicted of raping a white woman) or become the cause célèbre that gave the Scottsboro Boys pages of attention in books, magazines, and newspapers. However, this isn't to say the case was off the cultural radar screen altogether. An important discussion of the incident and the subsequent trials was written by Truman Nelson. This book, *The Torture of Mothers*, which he had to self-publish, was indispensable for Baldwin in his summaries, and it was from it that he gathered the often startling details.

What was to become a horrific tale began somewhat uneventfully. Some children rushing home from school and jostling one another inadvertently knocked over a fruit stand owned by Edward DeLuca, located at the corner of 128th Street and Lenox. A crate of grapefruit, after hitting the pavement, spilled onto the sidewalk. The children picked up a few and began to play catch with them. To stop the children and to regain his fruit, DeLuca blew a whistle. He was not aware that his whistle alerted members of a special tactical patrol that had been stationed in various basements throughout the community to offset what Mayor Robert Wagner believed was going to be "a long hot summer."

When Baldwin wrote that the children were "running from the police," it was these cops he was referring to, but, unfortunately, the children were not fast enough. Not only were they beaten mercilessly by policemen wielding billy clubs, but several adults, hoping to halt the brutal attack, themselves became victims. Frank Stafford, a black salesman, was one of those who sought to intervene and he was battered so severely that he lost an eye. Several local newspapers reported Stafford's recollection of what happened to him on the streets and later at the police precinct. He said more than thirty officers beat him and others who were under arrest. They came "into the room and started beating, punching us in the jaw, in the stomach, in the chest, beating us with a padded club," Stafford recalled. "They just beat us across the head bad, pulls us on the floor, spit on us, call us 'niggers, dogs, animals. You got what you deserve.'" In his report, Baldwin elaborated further:

> No one had, as yet, been charged with any crime. But the nightmare had not yet really begun. The salesman (Stafford) had been so badly beaten around one eye that it was found necessary to hospitalize him. Perhaps some sense of what it means to live in occupied territory can be suggested by the fact that the police took him to Harlem Hospital themselves—nearly nineteen hours after the beating. For fourteen days, the doctors at Harlem Hospital told him that they could do nothing for his eye, and he was removed to Bellevue Hospital, where for fourteen days, the doctors tried to save the eye. At the end of fourteen days it was clear that the bad eye could not be saved and was endangering the good eye. All that could be done, then, was to take the bad eye out.

The savage beating that Stafford and others received from this encounter, tragic as it was, had an even worse coda. Twelve days after "the Little Fruit Stand Riot," as it was popularly known, a white couple who owned a secondhand-clothing shop at 125th Street and Fifth Avenue was attacked in their store. The victims were Frank and Margit Sugar, Hungarian Jewish refugees. Mrs. Sugar, stabbed thirteen times, died from her wounds. A team of surgeons at Harlem Hospital was able to save her husband's life. "Within hours," wrote attorney Conrad Lynn, who would later represent one of the accused, "four of the six karate club members whom the police had identified at the scene of the Little Fruit Stand Riot were rounded up for questioning. Also picked up was a neighborhood ex-convict, Robert Barnes. A general alarm went out for Wallace Baker, only recently released from Harlem Hospital." Along with Baker, the police quickly arrested his friends—Daniel Hamm, William Craig, Ronald Felder, Walter Thomas, and Robert Rice, all of them teenagers. When it was clear that the young men were convenient scapegoats—and the NAACP and most elected officials in the district found the case too controversial—Lynn began to assemble a defense team to handle their trials. For Lynn, the arrests were too great a coincidence. William Kunstler, later to gain fame defending political activists such as the Chicago Seven was among the lawyers seeking to represent the youths. The lawyers had concluded that the accused were not going to get a vigorous defense from the court-appointed attorneys. It was this fact on which Lynn and his team would later base their appeals. "We were determined to make a constitutional issue of the denial of counsel of choice for two indigent defendants," Lynn explained in his autobiography, *There Is a Fountain.*

If Baldwin lacked the specific details of the inevitable railroading of the young men, he could speak to their plight in a way that none of the attorneys could. "My report," he said, adding that it was a plea for recognition of our common humanity, "is also based on what I myself know, for I was born in Harlem and raised there. Neither I, nor my family, can be said ever really to have left; we are—perhaps—no longer totally at the mercy of the cops and landlords as once we were: in any case, our roots, our friends, our deepest associations are there, and 'there' is only about fifteen blocks away." Indeed, both the vicious skirmish at DeLuca's stand and the bloody ordeal at the Sugars' store were well within Baldwin's extended neighborhood. Some of the menace of that area was displayed on national television that summer in a broadcast of *My Childhood*, a documentary that contrasted Baldwin's early years with those of Vice President Hubert Humphrey. Arthur Barron, the film's producer, hoped it would be different from the conventional documentaries, and it was.

In March 1965, the trial of the Harlem Six began. The accused could not have had a worse social and political atmosphere in which to be tried. It was a community still caught in the throes of hostility, mainly from nervous, trigger-happy white cops. One of them had shot and killed James Powell, a fifteen-year-old, in July 1964. Outraged by the death of the youth, hundreds of protesters marched on the 67th Precinct. A later demonstration outside the 28th Precinct on 123rd Street induced a swarm of policemen to attack the crowd, beating them with nightsticks and guns and dragging some of the demonstrators off to jail.

While Powell's killing occupied the minds of many Harlemites, Baldwin was still mourning the loss of Malcolm X and preparing to be immersed again into the civil rights movement as a participant in the Dr. King–led march from Selma to Montgomery. He could only give momentary attention to the Harlem Six, who in the first years of the case were also called the "Blood Brothers" or a "Blood Brotherhood." Their other moniker had been a cause of concern for Malcolm, who was traveling in Africa when a reporter asked him what he knew of them. According to a number of spurious stories, initiated by a black reporter for the *New York Times*, the six young men had sworn "blood oaths to murder white people." For the news media, it was a logical leap from them to the Nation of Islam, and then on to Malcolm, who by this time was no longer affiliated with the organization.

"In Lagos, I was greeted by Professor Essien-Udom of the Ibadan University, Malcolm recalled in his autobiography. "We were both happy to see each other. We had met in the United States as he had researched the Nation of Islam for his book, *Black Nationalism*. At his home, that evening, a dinner was held in my honor, attended by other professors, and professional people. As we ate, a young doctor asked me if I knew that New York City's press was highly upset about a recent killing in Harlem of a white woman—for which, according to the press, many were blaming me at least indirectly. . . . Some of these young Negroes, apprehended by the police, had described themselves as belonging to an organization called 'Blood Brothers.' These youths, allegedly, had said or implied that they were affiliated with 'Black Muslims' who had split away from the Nation of Islam to join up with me."

Malcolm informed his dinner guests that this was the first he had heard of the incident. None of violence, he said, came as a surprise to him, given the desperate living conditions that suffocated Blacks. "As for the 'Blood Brothers,'" he continued, "I said I considered all Negroes to be my blood brothers. I said the white man's efforts to make my name poison actually succeeded only in making millions of black people regard me like Joe Louis."

When Malcolm arrived home on May 21, he was besieged

by the largest press corps he had ever received. After dispatching reporters' questions about the Blood Brothers, he used the chance to excoriate white supremacy and America's pervasive racism. This moment was also an opportunity for him to expound on his travels and how visiting Mecca had transformed his understanding of Islam and universal brotherhood. "The press was glad to get rid of me that day," he said.

Neither Malcolm nor Baldwin noted that back in the 1920s there was another group called the African Blood Brotherhood, and they too were accused of swearing a blood oath of loyalty, with the overthrow of the United States their alleged violent intent. The group's stated purpose, according to Harry Haywood—who was a member of the organization for about six months—was to fight for "African liberation and redemption . . . and for the immediate protection and ultimate liberation of Negroes everywhere." Haywood wrote that it was a clandestine organization that never had a broad membership. The Harlem-based group never exceeded three thousand members. Most of its impact was felt through the *Crusader*, a news bulletin that at one time, Haywood claimed, had a circulation of 33,000. The influence of the organization had waned by the mid-twenties, but it somewhat inspired other communist and leftist formations.

Nearly a year later, Baldwin, despite the burden of illness, and working to complete a collection of short stories while weighing the details of a film company that was interested in his play *Blues for Mr. Charlie* as its first effort, had not forgotten the Harlem Six. Their plight was certainly on his mind in the winter of 1965 when he debated conservative thinker and journalist William F. Buckley, Jr. at Cambridge University in England before an audience of nearly a thousand students. Their topic was something that Baldwin had more than a passing acquaintance with—"The American Dream Is at the Expense of the American Negro." Clearly, the advantage was Baldwin's and he wasted no time warming to the task. Taking his text from the Bible, Baldwin invoked the Old Testament prophet Jeremiah: "I picked the cotton under someone else's whip for nothing . . . I carried it to the market. I built the railways . . ." The Southern oligarchy, Baldwin added, "was created by my labor, my sweat, the violation of my women, the murder of my children—all of this in the land of the free and the home of the brave." The remark was followed by wild applause.

As biographers W. J. Weatherby and David Leeming have observed, Baldwin put Buckley on the defensive, a position from which he never recovered, his high-sounding rhetoric making his argument all the more pedantic and ineffective. On several occasions the students hissed Buckley. When the tally was taken Baldwin received more than 500 "ayes," or favorable votes, to Buckley's 184 nays. But Baldwin's enjoyment of the victory was short-lived. Three days later he was informed that Malcolm had been assassinated.

By the summer of 1966, Baldwin began to see himself as a captive of the media but had little confidence in the reports, particularly those about him. In a letter to his brother, David, he warned that he would probably be in the news. "I don't want you to worry too much," he pled. "My activities on the part of the Harlem Six are bound to have repercussions, if they have not already. I suppose you saw my Report from Occupied Territory in *The Nation*. I have also drafted a petition—the petition is really a two-page version of my Report—

for international attention, and for signatures from people, prominent or otherwise, from all over the world."

In August 1967, Baldwin, now forty-three, while dividing his time between Paris and Istanbul was still campaigning for the boys' freedom. He delivered a blistering speech demanding a massive economic boycott in support of the Harlem Six, who by now had been imprisoned for more than two years. "The boys were convicted of first-degree murder," Baldwin wrote, "and are now ending their childhood and may end their lives in jail." Among the demands he voiced that evening before two thousand people at the Village Theater in lower Manhattan was for "Negroes" not to buy on credit and turn away "from General Motors. . . . If we cannot reach the American conscience, we must find some way of intimidating its self-interest." His good friend, Ossie Davis, was the event's master of ceremonies and singer Richie Havens performed. Funds were also being raised for civil rights work in Dorchester County, South Carolina.

In fact, the Six had been found guilty and sentenced to life imprisonment. As Lynn and his team had predicted, the appointed lawyers for the youth were terribly inadequate. But fortunately, as Lynn noted, the Supreme Court had abolished the death penalty while the trial was under way. "The case that was presented to the jury had been carefully constructed by the homicide assistants of District Attorney Frank Hogan," Lynn explained. "The circumstantial evidence heard by the jury was voluminous. The eyewitness testimony was skimpy, but it had not been shaken on cross-examination. Therefore, I remained convinced that the central issue on appeal had to be the denial of the choice of counsel." While

Lynn believed at least two of the convicted were innocent, mainly because of the coerced confessions and inconsistent argument from the prosecutors, Baldwin, like most Harlemites, felt all of them had been wrongly accused. "No one in Harlem," he wrote, "will ever believe that The Harlem Six are guilty–God knows their guilt has certainly not been proved. Harlem knows, though, that they have been abused and . . . possibly destroyed, and Harlem knows why–we have lived with it since our eyes opened on the world."

If the Harlem Six, the so-called Blood Brothers, were guilty, then Baldwin mused that we're all guilty. For him, the conviction of the Six was just another old-fashioned way of "getting bad niggers off the streets." Oddly, in the midst of a black nationalist upsurge in Harlem, the case didn't appear to attract great attention from some of the community's leading activists at that time. Most of the more prominent ones, including Amiri Baraka (LeRoi Jones), seemed to be more occupied on the cultural front, mounting theater projects, jam sessions, and poetry readings. "But we were on top of the case and many others like this where our children were being assaulted," said Elombe Brath, founder and president of the Patrice Lumumba Coalition. Brath also noted the support for the young men assembled by Carlos Cooks's African Nationalist Pioneer Movement.

Lynn, as we have seen, was an exception, although he was more to the left than the horde of cultural nationalists. The politically charged 1930s and a number of controversial cases had honed his analysis, and given him a perspective that was virtually unmatched among activists of his generation.

The same was true of Bill Epton and William McAdoo, and members of the Progressive Labor Party (PLP). Epton, a printer by trade, and McAdoo were leaders of the PLP and helped found the Harlem Defense Council, which was in the forefront of the struggle to free the Harlem Six. After they, along with Lynn, defied a court injunction to cease their demonstrations, Epton and McAdoo were arrested. Epton, the more vocal of the leaders, was charged with "criminal anarchy." He was later released on $10,000 bond, pending trial.

Three years after the Six were convicted, the appeal of the case from Lynn and his associates was heard. To their delight, the convictions were reversed. New trials were ordered, but Lynn and the other lawyers on his team were denied an opportunity to represent them. Two of the six were tried separately and found guilty and received life or long sentences. The other four defendants went on trial in February 1971.

By then Baldwin was nearly recovered from a bout of hepatitis. Troubling him most urgently, though, was the status of Angela Davis, who had been arrested for her alleged role in a shoot-out in San Rafael, California, in 1970. Davis, a member of the Communist Party, was charged with procuring the guns that Jonathan Jackson used in an attempted rescue of his brother George Jackson. The armed takeover of a courtroom ended in a fierce fire fight with the police, leaving Jonathan and several others dead, including the judge whom they had held as a hostage. Baldwin, as he had done for the Harlem Six, penned a letter in support of Davis that appeared in the *New York Review of Books* in January 1971. (Baldwin would express his anger again later in the year after George Jackson was killed in an alleged escape attempt from San Quentin Prison. Baldwin debunked the report by prison authorities, insisting to the press, "I don't believe any gun was smuggled to George Jackson. I think he was murdered in the prison.") Davis would later reprint Baldwin's letter as a preface to her book *If They Come in the Morning*, whose title was taken from Baldwin's last line in the letter: "For, if they take you in the morning, they will be coming for us that night." She was acquitted of kidnapping and murder charges in 1972.

A different fate awaited the Harlem Six—now reduced to four defendants. In the spring, the jury sent a note to the judge: they were deadlocked. Judge Frederick Backer declared a mistrial. Then another trial with a different judge ended in a deadlock. The appeal for bail was placed at $75,000 each, which, according to Lynn, was tantamount to no bail at all. Having already spent eight years in prison, the four were in no position to post a bond or to pay such an exorbitant amount. The only good news for the young men came on July 17, 1973. Robert Rice, represented by William Kunstler, and whose case had been separated from the others, was granted a new trial by a federal judge. "He said there was evidence to indicate that torture had been used to extract the confession, that Rice's fingerprint had been faked (and placed on the doorknob of the Sugars' store), and that the testimony of Robert Barnes had been perjured." Kunstler told reporter Akinshiju Ola of the *National Guardian* that it was Baldwin who brought him into the case. Like Baldwin, Kunstler, whose reputation as a radical lawyer would reach its apex with the Chicago Seven trial in the 1970s, grew up in Harlem and he and Baldwin would be participants in a number of radical causes, including an organization to abolish the House Un-American Activities Committee. Both attended DeWitt Clinton High School, though Kunstler was five years older than Baldwin. They would also be involved in seeking justice in the Atlanta child murders. Of particular note here is the so-called confession, which Baldwin elucidated in his essay. "A crime, as we know, is solved with someone arrested and convicted," he wrote. "It is not indispensable, but it is useful, to have a confession. If one is carried back and forth from the precinct to the hospital long enough one is likely to confess to anything."

In the spring and summer of 1974, Baldwin had a number of things to celebrate. First, there was his book *If Beale Street Could Talk*, a novel largely inspired by the ordeal of Tony Maynard. Maynard, a young black man, got entangled in a racially charged murder case, and since he was one of Baldwin's several "assistants," the author felt a need to come to his rescue. Second, during this same period Baldwin was awarded a centennial medal for being an "artist as prophet" from the Cathedral of St. John the Divine. Third, he marked his fiftieth birthday with friends at his residence in St. Paul de Vence in southern France. Fourth, and most joyously, Daniel Hamm was released from prison. Exiting prison, Hamm was greeted by all six of the mothers and by four of the others, who had been previously freed.

Despite the convictions and years in prison, most of the Six managed to salvage their lives. "They came away from it stronger than before," Lynn concluded. "Ronald Felder went to college. William Craig became a professional painter and writer. Walter Thomas was reunited with his wife and young son and works for an architectural firm. Daniel Hamm also went to college. Even poor Wallace Baker made the most of his gifts: he is a community street worker in Harlem." Not much has been written of the Six after this summation by

Lynn in the late seventies, and the fate of Robert Rice was still undecided.

Other than Lynn's reflections; a composition by Steve Reich, inspired by Hamm; Truman Nelson's book; and Baldwin's essay, there is little to commemorate the ordeal these young men endured. In 1980, director Woodie King, Jr. produced an hourlong docudrama, *The Torture of Mothers*, based on Nelson's book and featuring Ruby Dee, Clarise Taylor, Novella Nelson, Louise Stubbs, Sam Blue, and Walter Jones, with narration by Adolph Caesar. There is also a recording of Ossie Davis speaking out against the injustice of the case. The film, according to a blurb on the tape's case, is "brilliantly crafted around 25 hours of audio tape recorded by the mothers during their heroic effort." Literary and film critic Clyde Taylor summarized it as "restrained and naturalistic, and focuses on the mothers who are unable to comprehend why the legal system should crack down blindly on their sons."

"Now, what I have said about Harlem is true of Chicago, Detroit, Washington, Boston, Philadelphia, Los Angeles, and San Francisco—is true of every northern city with a large Negro population," Baldwin observed in his report, with a special eye toward the police brutality that had beaten confessions out of the Harlem Six. "And the police are simply hired enemies of this population. They are present to keep the Negro in his place and to protect white business interests, and they have no other function." And because they are hated, ignorant, and intimidated by the people, he added, "One cannot possibly arrive at a more surefire formula for cruelty."

What is incontrovertible is Baldwin's sense of justice and

fair play, his commitment to those snared by the so-called criminal justice system that consistently coaxed from him an unflinching righteous indignation. The plight of the Harlem Six, of Tony Maynard, and others obviously reminded him of the circumstances that dogged his youth, particularly those terrifying encounters with the white cops of Harlem, cops who seemed determined to make his occupied territory a living hell.

Chapter 8

The Jewish Question

There is no way to determine exactly when Baldwin became conscious of the Jewish population in Harlem; it may have occurred within moments of discovering that he was black. In 1921, three years before he was born, the Jewish population in Harlem, at some 180,000, was the third-largest in the world, according to the *Jewish Communal Register*. But in a little less than a decade it had decreased to about 5,000 north of 96th Street. Thus his adolescent years took place while his neighborhood underwent a rather dramatic transition. By the end of World War II, there were even fewer Jewish residents, since housing opportunities had become more plentiful elsewhere. The overall Jewish population in Harlem may have been appreciably reduced, but Jews still maintained a commanding presence in the business sector.

Baldwin's first knowledge of Jews or the Hebrew people—except for those who appeared at his apartment door demanding payments of some sort—was probably obtained from the Old Testament. Long before he learned and committed his Bible stories to memory, the plight of the Hebrew people and their struggle for freedom was part and parcel of African American history. The use of a heroic, uplifting tale about Abraham, Moses, Noah, Joshua, Daniel, Ruth, Samson, or Jesus was axiomatic, and no black preacher's sermon was complete without referring to at least one of them. More often than not, the Jews and their determination to be free from bondage was a useful example for black Americans to emulate. "We need to be more like Jews, see how they cling together and look out for each other," was a phrase that resounded in black communities and in Harlem. And if the ancient Jews, against the mighty armies of Pharaoh, could liberate themselves, then why not everyman?

Despite the adoration for the ancient Jews and their exemplary fight, an embrace of the contemporary Jews in Harlem was fraught with ambivalence. Some of that ambivalence was even heard from time to time among the Christian preachers who accused Jews of slaying the Son of God. And, perhaps even more distressing to the Jewish merchants and landlords living in close proximity to black residents in Harlem, they were categorically lumped in with the angst and hatred against whites in general. The syllogism would go something like this: Whitey was despised. Jews were white. So, Jews were despised. For black Americans the gatekeepers were just as guilty as the gate owners.

For "The Harlem Ghetto," an essay published in 1948 and discussed earlier in this book, Baldwin had been commissioned by *Commentary* magazine to write about the Harlem he knew. To a great extent in this essay, the Jews were excoriated, which subsequently was the source of relentless charges that Baldwin was anti-Semitic. "Jews in Harlem are small tradesmen, rent collectors, real estate agents and pawn brokers; they operate in accordance with the American business tradition of exploiting Negroes, and they are therefore identified with oppression and are hated for it," he charged. Baldwin, in effect, came out swinging and with no intention of taking any prisoners or constraining the venom that he had, no doubt, heard over and over again while coming of age in the community. There was a reason some black Americans hated Jews, he insisted (noting his own weakness in this regard), and it had nothing to do with their Jewishness. "When the Negro hates the *Jew as a Jew* he does so partly because the nation does and in much the same painful fashion as he hates himself," he explained.

If Baldwin was anti-Semitic, it certainly found no expression during his teen years at DeWitt Clinton High School, when his best friends and associates on the *Magpie* were Jews, including Emile Capouya, Richard Avedon, and Sol Stein, all of whom would have enduring relationships with him and help to further his literary career. (Jess Rand, another classmate, who later became a publicist for Sammy Davis, Jr., might also be added to this list.) In his memoir, which focused on his lifelong friendship with Baldwin, Sol Stein made no reference to any hostility between the two of them; there is no indication that Baldwin might have at any time disliked Stein because he was a Jew. The two often dined together; sometimes Baldwin ate at his home and sometimes Stein had dinner with the Baldwins. "Baldwin and I came to our friendship with differences," Stein recalled in his memoir. "He was black and I was white, he loved men and I loved women, he assumed his ancestors came to America in chains, and I assumed my parents, who slipped over the border separately and illegally, came here because they had nowhere else to go. Despite the differences—we lived many miles apart—because of our friendship our families took a liking to each other."

It was Stein, Baldwin confessed, who pushed and prodded him to collect his essays in *Notes of a Native Son*, and who would later collaborate with him on a television play, which was never produced. The closest either of them came to discussing anything remotely related to blacks and Jews is at the end of a letter Baldwin wrote to Stein in 1956, where he refers to the name of Leland Dana, one of Stein's children, suggesting that her name "must be an old Hebrew name."

Baldwin had an equally close relationship to Emile Capouya, who traced his Jewish heritage through his immigrant parents from Spain and Russia. Capouya, in many respects, was closer to Baldwin than Stein since it was Capouya who introduced Baldwin to Beauford Delaney, later to become the writer's most significant muse. He also helped Baldwin get a job where he worked laying railroad track for the army in Belle Mead, New Jersey. Capouya related to one of Baldwin's biographers that Baldwin tended "to see everything in biblical terms," often citing the New and Old Testaments to support his arguments. "It often annoyed him that his friends, several of them skeptical Jewish intellectuals, were not as impressed with his biblical references as he was." To some degree, these encounters might have been pivotal in Baldwin's later decision to abandon the church and leave the preaching behind.

As for Richard Avedon, his other schoolmate and acclaimed photographer, he and Baldwin were reunited in 1963. Baldwin supplied the text to *Nothing Personal*, a collection of Avedon portraits of various people, famous and ordinary. The text here was typically Baldwinesque, replete with stunning lyricism, and, in contrast to the title, deeply personal. To give the photos additional ballast—and the blurred image of Malcolm X and the overpowering closeups of Bertrand Russell and Martin Luther King III are particularly memorable—Baldwin observed how the pictures were reminiscent of his own nights and days coming of age in Harlem. Among his concluding words: "For nothing is fixed, forever, forever, forever, it is not fixed; the earth is always shifting, the light is always changing, the sea does not cease to grind down the rock. Generations do not cease to be born, and we are responsible to them because we are the only witnesses they have."

Baldwin never said explicitly which of his three close Jewish friends it was who came to his home one day, almost to experience firsthand his stepfather's unbridled wrath. It may have been Capouya. "My best friend in high school was a Jew," Baldwin related in *The Fire Next Time*. "He came to our house once, and afterward my father asked, as he asked everyone, 'Is he a Christian?'—by which he meant 'Is he saved?' I really do not know whether my answer came out of innocence or venom, but I said coldly. 'No. He's Jewish.' My father slammed me across the face with his great palm, and in that moment everything flooded back—all the hatred and all the fear, and the depth of merciless resolve to kill my father rather than allow my father to kill me . . . I told my father, 'He's a better Christian than you are,' and walked out of the house."

Apparently Baldwin never told Capouya, Stein, or Avedon about this incident. However, all of them must have, in one way or the other known of his dislike for his stepfather. "He had a curious respect for the man, and, at the same time, a terrible resentment," Capouya told Fern Eckman. "And what was so odd in so young a boy was that he had pity for him. Jimmy recognized the economic and psychological and moral and spiritual trap his father was in. He spoke of him as someone you couldn't like but had to respect."

The years between high school and his first major essay gave him ample opportunity to interact in a more studied way with the Jews around him. To find the largest congregations of blacks and Jews was easy: just survey the several leftist organizations. Interracial cooperation between blacks and Jews found its best example in the Communist Party. Such prominent activists A. Philip Randolph, Benjamin Davis, Max Yergan, Paul Robeson, Claudia Jones, Abner Berry, James Ford, Howard "Stretch" Johnson, and Doxey Wilkerson gave radical politics an attractive panache, and these prestigious citizens were affiliated with a number of political formations that were allied with Jewish organizations and institutions. "In 1946 the American Jewish Congress created the Commission on Law and Social Action, which was to draft many of the bills against racial and religious discrimination, and whose frequent collaboration with the NAACP constituted the basis of the Black-Jewish alliance in the civil rights movement," wrote Martha Biondi in her book that thoroughly examined the struggle for civil rights in postwar New York City. And few evoked the alliance between blacks and Jews more fervently than Benjamin Davis, a member of the Communist Party, who succeeded Adam Clayton Powell as councilman from Harlem. Discussing the rights of African Americans during his campaign for council in the early forties, Davis warned his listeners that "jim-crowism and anti-Semitism are weapons which do Hitler's work."

Because of his long association with Jews and his growing penchant for activism, it is easy to see how Baldwin slowly gravitated toward militant politics. For a very brief time, not too long after graduating from high school, he was a member of the Young Communist League or the Young People's Socialist League, depending on which biographer you trust. "By the time I was nineteen, I was a Trotskyite [a follower of Leon Trotsky] having learned a great deal by then, if not about communism, at least about Stalinists." And while Baldwin's tenure was of little consequence to his ideological development—eventually adopting a kind of radical Democratic stance—he was certainly aware, perhaps from his teachers or his classmates at DeWitt Clinton High School, of the political differences between the organizations, and if he had to choose one or the other he might have preferred the notion of permanent worldwide revolution espoused by the Trotskyites over the communism in one nation promoted by the Stalinists. It seems that Baldwin was never much of an ideologue, possessing only a vague notion of the differing political parties and philosophical tendencies, though he was by no means naïve to the cynicism of power politics or the machinations of the various political groups that eagerly pursued him. During an interview in 1972 with Joe Walker of the newspaper *Muhammad Speaks*, he was asked if socialism would ever come to America. "I would think so," he answered. "I don't see any other way for it to go. But you have to be very careful what you mean by socialism. When I use the word I'm not thinking about Lenin for example." Nor was he thinking very definitively about the difference between socialism and Lenin's communist vision during this interview, which varies from his keener analysis in the pages of *No Name in the Street.*

By the late forties, Baldwin had cut his literary teeth on nearly all the leading journals and magazines on the left with his book reviews. Even more enduring was his introduction and conversations with Richard Wright. Wright, then the most famous black writer in the country, had come to Harlem at the request of the Communist Party in 1937 and was an editor at the *Daily World* and the *New Challenge.* But by the time he met Baldwin in 1945, he was no longer a member of the Communist Party, leaving it after struggling to reconcile his individual, artistic expression with the collective demands of the Party. Though eventually Wright and Baldwin's relationship would become strained, Wright provided a substantial push, accelerating Baldwin's novelist dreams. Three years later, the nascent novelist Baldwin was being praised as the emerging essayist after *Commentary*, a journal published by the American Jewish Committee, contracted him to write about a community he knew so well.

The black media, some black leaders, housing projects, the church, and the Jews of Harlem were all gathered and skewered on Baldwin's revolving spit. Within days of its publication in 1948, "The Harlem Ghetto" was the talk of the town, outraging hordes of Harlemites. Folks were furious at his exaggerations, and felt he had vastly overstated his case. Most upset were the Jews; however, Raymond Rosenthal, the editor of the journal, was ecstatic over the essay. "It was a masterpiece," he said, noting how well it was accepted by everyone at the publication. Whatever the case, and however roiled blacks and Jews were about his opinions, Baldwin wasn't around long enough to accept the praise or to avoid the aspersion. By November 11, his bags were packed and he was on his way to Paris, leaving a herd of scapegoats behind.

Over the succeeding years, there was very little commentary from Baldwin about blacks and Jews, until the late sixties, when a bitter dispute between black and white members of the Student Nonviolent Coordinating Committee had practically ruptured that civil rights organization. Even from as far away as France, Baldwin knew of the bitterness that had divided them. The chant of "Black Power!" had created irreconcilable turmoil in the civil rights movement, and, inevitably, it would affect other aspects of society. A tipping point came in 1967 when the *Liberator* magazine (which shouldn't be confused with a magazine of the same name in the 1920s edited by Max Eastman, or *Liberation* magazine, the pacifist journal under the watchful eye of A. J. Muste, mentioned earlier) published an article titled "Anti-Semitism in the Black Ghetto." Baldwin was again embroiled in controversy since he, like Ossie Davis, was on the magazine's advisory board.

As before, the clamor and indignation from the Jewish community—even the American Jewish Committee, which had cheered his "The Harlem Ghetto"—was expressed derisively, with a strong demand of retractions and for Baldwin to disassociate himself from the magazine. Baldwin immediately wrote a letter to the magazine's editor, Daniel Watts, asking that his name be removed from the masthead and that his letter be published. Watts removed his name but refused to publish the letter. "They were forced to quit because of economic pressure by Jews," Watts contended, adding that Davis never contributed an article to the magazine "he was too busy writing for white publications." The letter was later published by *Freedomways* magazine, and Baldwin composed another article based on it, which he titled "Negroes Are Anti-Semitic Because They're Anti-White." In many respects the article was déjà vu, "The Harlem Ghetto" rehashed.

Baldwin began the article by explaining why blacks in Harlem hated Jews. "We hated them because they were terrible landlords, and did not take care of the building," he wrote. Not all the Jews or white people were bad, he quickly noted. Even so, "It is bitter to watch the Jewish storekeeper locking up his store for the night, and going home," he asserted. "Going, with your money in his pocket, to a clean neighborhood, miles from you, which you will not be allowed to enter. Nor can it help the relationship between most Negroes and most Jews when part of this money is donated to civil rights."

This response was a bit stronger than his letter in *Freedomways* in which he wrote that "it is immoral, to blame Harlem on the Jew."

The *Liberator*, launched in 1961, was a multiracially owned magazine, but the owners apparently never intervened to determine the direction of the publication. "Allegedly," wrote Harold Cruse, "Jewish liberalism too was involved in the corporate ownership, but this influence was never exerted editorially." Davis's and Baldwin's roles as advisors to the *Liberator* were never clearly defined, and after the brouhaha over anti-Semitism, Watts dropped the twelve-member board, which included Richard B. Moore and George Murphy, both significant political voices in Harlem and black America.

In Cruse's estimation, the straw that finally broke the "pro-nationalist" *Liberator's* back was a review that warmly praised Lorraine Hansberry's play *The Sign in Sidney Brustein's Window*. The reviewer felt the play was lacking in black nationalistic fervor: "The play is concerned with the necessity of making an active decision about what one's duty will be in the face of evil and corruption. Miss Hansberry chose an idealistic Jewish bohemian as the character who must make this decision." Such a choice is not so far-fetched when you consider that Hansberry's husband, Bob Nemiroff, was Jewish. But for Cruse this choice was next to anathema, and it symbolized the magazine's spineless capitulation to Jewish influence and power in the theater. "In any event," Cruse asserted, "to see today a Negro stage writer bending over backwards to glorify the Jewish image in the face of the rising tide of color, seeking new social status and new identification in world culture, is to witness a cultural phenomenon nothing short of a political sellout."

Hansberry's "sellout," Cruse lamented, was typical of the "brainwashed, self-repudiation complex of the Negro intellectual," and by inference he included Baldwin, for whom his vitriol flowed incessantly. This damnation of the "Harlem left-wing literary and cultural elite" is a loud and consistent theme throughout Cruse's book, and Baldwin is assailed as a leader of the assembly. We are left to speculate how Baldwin felt about his fellow autodidact—notwithstanding his flaws— who was so relentlessly critical of his colleagues. But Cruse chose to sit in the back of the room taking notes, only to use them years later in his lengthy book of diatribe. Baldwin did have something to say about Hansberry and the play, however. "It is possible, for example, that *The Sign in Sidney*

Brustein's Window attempts to say too much; but it is also exceedingly probable that it makes so loud and uncomfortable a sound because of the surrounding silence; not many plays, presently, risk being accused of attempting to say too much." Graciously, and with his usual way of speaking paradoxically, Baldwin pledged his allegiance to Hansberry, whom he sincerely adored despite their sometimes sustained arguments over artistic differences. In an interview with the *Black Scholar* magazine, he said that Hansberry "was like my baby sister, in a way. I can't think of her without a certain amount of pain."

In 1979, in a letter ostensibly composed to defend Ambassador Andrew Young, who, under pressure for meeting with Palestinian leaders, had resigned his position at the United Nations, Baldwin once more felt compelled to elaborate on Jewish history, even reaching back to show how the discovery of America coincided with the Inquisition and the expulsion of Jews from Spain. More to the point, he returned to those early days in Harlem: "The first white man I ever saw was the Jewish manager who arrived to collect the rent, and he collected the rent because he did not own the building. I never, in fact, saw any of the people who owned any of the buildings in which we scrubbed and suffered so long, until I was a grown man and famous. None of them were Jews." Furthermore, the Jews could not be blamed for doing the "usurious dirty work" of Christians. Baldwin said he knew a murderer when he saw one, "and the people who were trying to kill me were not Jews."

Not only were Jews not out to kill him, he insisted, they often came to his rescue, and Baldwin presented examples of this both in his essays and in his short stories. It was a Jewish friend who sneaks a black man into his room in "Previous Condition," his first piece of published fiction, only to be discovered by the landlady who tells him that no colored people are allowed in the apartment. The man flees to Harlem but soon, like Baldwin, finds safety and comfort in Greenwich Village.

Baldwin was sometimes forced to dredge up all sorts of memories to prove he wasn't anti-Semitic. For example, in *No Name in the Street*, he relates an incident where a young Jewish man fried his wife's afterbirth in a pan and then ate it. "He never knew it," Baldwin said of the man, but "I loved him, and the silence between us was the precise indication of how deeply something in me responded to, and is still bewildered by, his trouble." Baldwin also expressed an abiding admiration, if not love, for Norman Mailer, and for all the anticipated fireworks from their encounters, particularly on the issues of blacks and Jews, there was nary a spark. "I am a black boy from the Harlem streets, and Norman is a middle-class Jew," Baldwin wrote in "The Black Boy Looks at the White Boy," and this description was the extent of any possible ethnic or racial animosity from either of them. They would encounter each other again in Chicago on September 25, 1962, when they were assigned—Mailer for *Esquire* and Baldwin for *Nugget*—to cover the heavyweight championship bout between Floyd Patterson and challenger Sonny Liston. At ringside the two writers were separated by a vacant seat (though one writer has Baldwin between Mailer and Ben Hecht), which minimized any possibility of exchanges in the crowded Comiskey Park. They didn't have to tolerate each other very long because Liston vanquished Patterson in two minutes and twenty seconds of the first round. Like the fighters, the two writers went their separate ways with Baldwin $750 lighter since he had placed his bet on Patterson. Baldwin was probably also still stewing from Mailer's nasty comments about *Another Country*, published that summer. Mailer had dismissed it as "abominably written." To add a little more vinegar to the blister, Mailer charged that Saul Bellow, a Jewish writer, in his book *Henderson the Rain King*, had plumbed deeper into the black man's psyche than had Baldwin.

One final anecdote to the Baldwin-Mailer melodrama comes from an interview with Baldwin by Quincy Troupe. This was the last interview Baldwin gave before his death. Baldwin said that one of his siblings, from his father's first wife, lived with Mailer while he was writing his essay *The White Negro*. "He was taking pages out of Mailer's typewriter," Baldwin said, "changing his clothes—they wore the same clothes, exchanged cars, and his car was better than Norman's at the time. He was like a second husband in a way. They lived together. They lived close together. Norman doesn't know I know this. No one knows this." Baldwin said the encounter took place in the thirties and the early forties in California, which means Mailer wrote it many years before it was published in 1957. Mailer had no idea he was living with one of Baldwin's stepbrothers while he was writing a book about Black Americans. His name was Osby Mitchell.

(Gloria Karefa-Smart, Baldwin's sister, takes exception to this account, doubting whether the sequence of events ever occurred. I was unable to independently verify the matter but since it was quoted by Baldwin to Troupe, the editor and I agreed to let it stand with this caveat.)

In an interview with me, Troupe recalled an incident with

Baldwin and Jews during an appearance by Baldwin at the College of Staten Island, where Troupe taught and Baldwin had been invited. "It was sometime during the early eighties, I'm not exactly sure when, and I was asked by the president of the college, Edmond Volpe, if I could get Jimmy to come," he began. "I told him I'd try. When I called Jimmy and told him about it, he agreed but a fee he stipulated was nonnegotiable, plus he wanted a car for round-trip service." Everything was going all right, Troupe continued, until Baldwin made a comment in support of the Palestinians. "A good percentage of the audience was composed of Jews, and when Jimmy said that he set off a firestorm. Hands were raised and people wanted to know how he could support the Palestinians. Jimmy refused to buckle down under the assault. He told them that the land settled by Israeli people belonged to the Palestinians and he compared their plight with the decimation of the American Indians in this country. Jimmy was vehemently defending his position when practically half the audience got up and left." Troupe said he believed his denial of promotion to a full professor was directly attributable to the incident. "Instead of faulting me, they should have gone after the president; it was his decision to bring him," he said. President Volpe's invitation to Baldwin may have stemmed from their mutual interest in the work of William Faulkner.

Baldwin's contretemps at the College of Staten Island or with Mailer did not have the same effect on him or his standing in Harlem as did the withering personal and professional attack from Harold Cruse. The mere fact that he had incurred the enmity and wrath of Cruse was reason enough to believe that Baldwin didn't hate Jews, since Cruse did have more than a few bones to pick with the Jews of New York City.

Furthermore, Cruse himself exonerated Baldwin, whom he defines as an "innocent and provincial intellectual," declaring that "it would not be correct to call Baldwin a Jew-lover, inasmuch as Baldwin simply loves everybody, even those he feels are against him. More exactly, he fits the category of an apologist for the Jews, true to the tradition of Negro ex-preachers well-versed in Hebrew biblical lore and all that deep-river-waters-of-Jordan history."

If Baldwin, as Cruse states, loved everybody, then by logic he loved Cruse, too, though in Cruse Baldwin had a deter-mined adversary, someone who at every turn sought to destroy him. As Baldwin made it patently clear, the people trying to kill him were not Jews.

Though they might not have been trying to kill him, some of them must have cringed when reading *Tell Me How Long the Train's Been Gone.* Twenty years after his essay with its harsh pronouncements on the presence of Jews in Harlem, Jews were mercilessly assailed in the 1968 novel. "We all hated Rabinow-itz with a perfectly exquisite hatred," is the derision cast upon the landlord by Leo Proudhammer, the book's narrator. The landlord, he tells us, took his time about fixing broken win-dows, gave them no heat in the winter, and threatened daily to put them out of the apartment on "their collective ass." And there is Mr. Shapiro, the grocer, who unlike the butcher, is occasionally kind and extends black residents credit. "Can't you see that Jew's hand is all over the scale?" exclaims Leo's brother, Caleb. And Caleb's enmity is inherited from his father, who believes the Jews controlled the film industry and deliber-ately set out to mess up black people's minds with the films. "You don't know the Jew like I know him," Leo and Caleb's father declares. His attitude is very similar to one expressed by a minor character in *Just Above My Head*. In a dialogue with Arthur Montana in that story, Red spits out a stream of invectives about Jews. "You want me to peddle my ass to them Jew crackers," he screamed. "That's why black people is where they is today! Always sucking around the fucking Jew! Them bastards had my ass in a vise one time and they can't have it no more! I'm going to make me some money!"

Caleb's mother, however, is of another mind, ridiculing her husband for his narrow-mindedness, "you don't never go to see them [films]."

But none of this anti-Semitism from the Proudhammers disturbed the reviewer at *Commentary*, who concluded it was a "masterpiece." Others not only deemed the book less than masterful, they questioned, as they had on many other occasions, Baldwin's ability to keep his fictional tone free of what was a reality for him. Could he, for example, keep it out of his public addresses, his classroom guest lectures? Apparently not, if Julius Lester is right about his accusation that Baldwin made anti-Semitic statements while addressing his class at the University of Massachusetts at Amherst during the academic year of 1983–84. That speech, almost in its entirety, was reprinted in *Black Scholar* in 1988. There is a question-and-answer session in which Baldwin spends a considerable amount of time defending the Reverend Jesse Jackson, who, according to the *Washington Post* in early 1984, often used such words as "Hymie" and "Hymietown" (for New York City) when talking to reporters. Baldwin also found it necessary to explain exactly what he meant about Jews doing the "dirty work of Christians," a term he often used when discussing the relationship between blacks and Jews. "The people who own Harlem, for example, never arrive to collect the rent," he said, implying that the Jew collecting the rent does not own the apartment building. "The people who are really responsible for the misery all up and down those streets do not run the pawn shop. The people responsible for the horror are in the liquor store . . ." The owners of the things in Harlem, he continued, did not live in Harlem but in "Croton-on-the-Hudson. Or it was Columbia University. The people who own anything, who really own it in the ghetto, are not to be found in the ghetto. The middleman is in the ghetto doing, in fact, the Christian's dirty work." This remark was met with strong applause from the audience.

Baldwin was clearly upset over the anti-Semitic accusation and so was the UMass Afro-American Studies Department, which quickly produced a pamphlet denying the allegation and supporting Baldwin. Nor was Baldwin pleased with Lester, an Afro-American who had converted to Judaism—much in the manner of Sammy Davis, Jr., who like Baldwin was born in Harlem and who denied that anti-Semitism was widespread in America. Baldwin was deeply offended by the hostile attitude Lester displayed during their interview for the *New York Times Book Review*. But rather then being rankled by discussion about Jews, the two hit a serious snag during their exchanges about the merit of William Styron's novel *The Confessions of Nat Turner*. In addition, Baldwin made comments about Norman Mailer that Lester believed were nothing more than an "eloquent evasion." "I don't want to talk about Norman," Baldwin told Lester. "I know much more about Norman than I'm willing to say in print," he continued, perhaps alluding to the fact that one of his stepbrothers was once closely associated with Mailer. This response by Baldwin about Mailer reveals once more the difficulty he had avoiding the Jewish question, though as we've seen earlier in this chapter, he did choose a moment in his last interview to disclose what he knew of Mailer. It was a parting shot to his old adversary, whose response, as Baldwin probably knew, would come too late to have any lasting effect.

Baldwin, like so many of his more politically conscious friends and colleagues, made a distinction between his feelings about Jews and about Zionism. Zionism, symbolized by the state of Israel, was unacceptable and equivalent to imperialism and racism. Yet Baldwin's play *The Amen Corner* was highly acclaimed in Tel Aviv; some Israelis were apparently willing to set aside their differences with Baldwin. When the final curtain went down on August 8, 1965, Claudia McNeil (who played Sister Margaret) was greeted with a wave of "bravos." "We seldom see these days uninhibited dramatics which sounded at all times sincere," a reviewer gushed in the *Jerusalem Post*. Baldwin had arrived two hours before the play was over and after being beckoned to the stage and introduced by McNeil, received warm applause. How much of this might have been a reaction to McNeil's curtain speech, which she delivered using a few Yiddish expressions, one can only speculate. She also told a heartfelt story about the memory of her foster parents, who were Jewish. In any case, it was a moment that Baldwin truly relished, and it may have helped in his effort to stay in the good graces of the Jewish people, no matter where they lived.

Six years later, in 1971, Baldwin faced a troubling situation with a Jewish editor, Shlomo Katz, of *Midstream*, a monthly Jewish review. Katz charged that he had been taken off *The David Frost Show* at the last minute because Baldwin had objected to appearing with him. Katz claimed that he was scheduled to appear for a taping of the show with Baldwin and Margaret Mead; Baldwin and the famed anthropologist had just published a book together, *A Rap on Race.* The discussion, Katz said, was to be focused on racial issues, and he and Baldwin had conducted such a session in his magazine and elsewhere. He was told, through a spokesman for the show, that Baldwin had said, "I will not discuss this issue with him." There was no response from Baldwin. It was disclosed that Baldwin was only made aware of Katz's appearance until a half-hour before the taping. The spokesman for Frost said that both men would be invited to appear on another program. But that never happened.

Some of the feud between Katz and Baldwin may have stemmed from earlier encounters between them. When Baldwin's "An Open Letter to My Sister, Miss Angela Davis," appeared in the *New York Times Review of Books* in January 1971, Katz was angered by an analogy in which Baldwin viewed Davis's predicament as akin to a "Jewish housewife in a boxcar headed for Dachau . . ." While there was no explicit citing of the Holocaust, Katz was infuriated by the comparison. And this residue of dissention could probably be traced back even further to 1964 when Katz was a commentator, but not a panelist on the aforementioned roundtable on liberalism, sponsored by *Commentary* magazine. There is a wider and valuable discussion on this matter and others related to blacks and Jews in Emily Miller Budick's highly informative *Blacks and Jews in Literary Conversation* (Cambridge University Press, 1998, pages 79 and 105). Of particular note is Budick's dissection of *The Fire Next Time,* and I agree that the text is as much scripture as it is historical and a cultural narrative, with deep theological roots.

For Baldwin and Mead, there were moments when they vehemently disagreed about Christians and Jews. Baldwin had made the point, as he often did, that the Jews seldom owned the buildings where they picked up the rent. Mead challenged this, insisting that there were times when the Jews did own the buildings. A portion of their exchange follows:

Baldwin: Well, that's what I meant when I said the Jews were still doing the Christians' dirty work. For example, in Harlem, the man who owns the building in which you live—

Mead: You know, this isn't true in the United States anymore.

Baldwin: It's true.

Mead: Oh, fiddlesticks!

Baldwin: No, Margaret, I was there.

Mead: Look, the Jews owned it.

Baldwin: The Jew was the landlord, but the Christian owned the land; the Christian owned the building.

Mead: Sometimes and sometimes not.

Baldwin: The man who owned the building—

Mead: It may have been Trinity Church, I know, but I—

Baldwin: Precisely. The man who owned the building did not arrive to collect the rent. The Jew was the middleman.

Mead: Or Columbia University. Or Syrians.

Baldwin: It doesn't make any difference.

Mead: Wait. Wait. It does make a difference. These are the facts that make a difference.

Baldwin: In our case it was the Jew.

Mead: Yep, I know, but you said—

Baldwin: Now, I know this is a very dangerous conversation, and let me try to clean it up a little bit. I don't want to get sidetracked on anti-Semitism. My only point is a very simple one: That before the American Jew or the Jewish American is a Jew he is an American, like anybody else in this country, and the crisis for me is whether or not we will be able to overcome the uses to which we have been put and become something resembling a people, instead of several tribes, because that is what we still are.

Chapter 9

Harlem, Real and Imagined

To a great degree, Harlem tended to be just another character for Baldwin: he treated it with the same brush of contradictions he used on his other subjects. For the most part, though, Harlem was typecast as the lowlife harlot, consistently present in his nonfiction and only occasionally beautified in his fiction.

Baldwin's first notable compositions, *Go Tell It on the Mountain* and "The Harlem Ghetto," essentially mirror each other. The essay was published first and because his fiction tended to veer close to the realties of his life, it was almost impossible for him to avoid the depressing squalor and poverty that confronted him daily. Beginning with these two Baldwin classics, we'll see in this chapter the similarity—and sometimes dissimilarity—between his fiction and nonfiction in their depictions of Harlem.

The opening sentence of "The Harlem Ghetto" sets the descriptive tone of a beat-down Harlem; it will be a relentless one-note theme of decay and despair, forcing you to wonder when and how Harlem was that powerful magnet attracting people from all over the world. "Harlem, physically at least, has changed very little in my parents' lifetime or in mine," Baldwin begins. "Now as then the buildings are old and in desperate need of repair, the streets are crowded and dirty, and there are too many human beings per square block."

A Harlem overflowing with residents, and with more apparently on their way, brings to mind a quip by Yogi Berra: "Nobody goes there anymore because it's too crowded." Since the turn of the twentieth century Harlem has shown a steady growth of population. In 1939, just about the time Baldwin was entering puberty, New York City's black population reached 458,444, making it the largest concentration of black Americans, and the bulk of this number lived in Harlem. It was this crowd that seemed magnified each time Baldwin tried to negotiate the streets from home to P.S. 139.

In Baldwin's essay, other than the need to demand a better education, nothing is said about the educational system or the schools. He ridicules the black press, slams black leadership, who are created and defeated by the same circumstances, denounces the projects, and spends far too much time discussing the Jews and the impossibility of any kind of constructive relationship between them and their black neighbors.

If Baldwin composed the essay to draw fire, he got even more than he wished for. And given his emphasis on the dirt and filth of Harlem, the community would seem to have been an ideal prospect for Title I funding under the Federal Housing Act that was passed within months of the essay's publication. But the "slum clearance" funds, which developer Robert Moses used to construct low-income projects, were not earmarked for Harlem. Nor was Moses's plan to build an expressway across Harlem from river to river.

Go Tell It on the Mountain mentions Harlem only a few times, though it is clear that most of the urban scenes, in which storefront churches figure prominently, are in Harlem. The descriptions of a Harlem that Baldwin knew so well may have been limited by distance, since he wrote most of the book while living abroad. In addition, most of the book takes place indoors, except for the pastoral scenes in a southern town, which could have been somewhere near New Orleans, from where Baldwin's stepfather (or Gabriel, in *Go Tell It on the Mountain*) migrated.

In Baldwin's fiction the shadow of Harlem sometimes hovers even when he's describing some other city. In *Go Tell It on the Mountain*, his description of a town in New Jersey ("the nigger part of town") could have been about Harlem, or at least modeled on it. So, at the very beginning of his career as a professional writer, whether in his fiction or non-fiction, Harlem was often depicted as squalid, an absolutely dreadful place to live.

As in *Go Tell It on the Mountain*, in *The Amen Corner*, Baldwin's first play, Harlem is taken for granted, and while it is alluded to, it is never mentioned per se. The play is in many respects merely a dramatization of the church scenes that appear in the novel. It was, in effect, a companion piece to the novel, one that would gestate for twelve years before it was produced and subsequently rewritten. Harlem is inferred in act two when Brother Boxer relates that David, much like John Grimes in the novel, has been spending some of his Sundays in local bars. "And just this very evening, not five minutes ago, I seen him down on 125th Street with some white horn player . . ."

By 1950, Baldwin was broke in Paris, and to make ends

meet he recycled some of his earlier works to a number of magazines. *New Story*, a freshly minted magazine, published "The Outing," a short story about a church's annual summer retreat on July 4th. (It's unlikely Baldwin titled it to suggest "outing" a gay person, since there's little in the story to denote any homosexuality, except perhaps at the end when Johnnie seeks comfort from David by resting his head on his shoulders. Nor can it be said with any certainty if the term "outing" was used at that time.) Parts of this story would appear in *Go Tell It on the Mountain* and *The Amen Corner*, and once again Harlem is never more present than by its absence. It's clear that the church members are temporarily fleeing the community, looking for some relief from the intense environment. The descriptions of the country scenes stand in stark contrast to the hustle and bustle of Harlem; the mountain greenery opposes the dull, dirty gray that made the neighborhood so depressing. Bear Mountain, up the Hudson River, seems here a long way from Harlem, and that distance from Baldwin's early stomping grounds reminds one of the author's flight away from the city to Paris, and his quest to leave behind the demonic trappings of home.

That irrepressible ghetto, an invisible metaphor in his novels, is fully fleshed out in "Notes of a Native Son." This essay (a collection bears the same title) was mostly a reflective piece in which Baldwin recalled his father's funeral and the riot of 1943. Twelve years after his father's death and the riot, he still had sharp memories of those events. Much of what he wrote then is similar to his earlier impressions of Harlem, summoning once again the pain and disgust at the core of "The Harlem Ghetto." It was the smashing of things— not only the need for Harlem to smash something, "a chronic need," he wrote, but the sound and fury of ghetto members smashing themselves. But, as he noted, there will come a time when the various modes of letting off steam by battering one another will not suffice. "If ever, indeed, the violence which fills Harlem's churches, pool halls, and bars erupts outward in a more direct fashion, Harlem and its citizens are likely to vanish in an apocalyptic flood," he wrote. "That this is not likely to happen is due to a great many reasons, most hidden and powerful among them the Negroes' real relation to the white American." And that relationship, Baldwin contended, prohibited something as uncomplicated and satisfactory as pure hatred. Perhaps it wasn't pure hatred, but the community exploded in anger nine years later.

From 1948 to 1956, when *Giovanni's Room* was published, Baldwin had spent most of his time in Europe, mainly in Paris. His love for Paris is evident on every other page, while Harlem is a long-ago memory and isn't mentioned at all. And without Harlem there is a shift in the style of his prose, as James Campbell noted: "the bright prose which had made vivid the sphere of Harlem worship turns to soupy lyricism when transposed to cafes in the Paris dawn."

On the one occasion when the narrator, David, one of Baldwin's stock names, refers to New York City, it is to indicate his fondness for Manhattan; otherwise the story has one glowing report on Paris after another. Even the squat chimney stacks of Paris are "beautiful and varicolored under a pearly sky." And later, more effusively: "The multitude of Paris seems to be dressed in blue every day but Sunday, when, for the most part, they put on an unbelievably festive black. Here they were now, in blue, disputing, every inch, our passage, with their wagons, handtrucks, camions, their bursting baskets carried at an angle steeply self-confident on the back."

Nonetheless, for all the alluring blues, pretty springs, and cognac galore, there are moments when David yearns to go home, not to his hotel, where unpaid bills awaited him, but "home across the ocean, to things and people I knew and understood." Giovanni, his lover, is at home, and belongs to Paris, but the strange city does not belong to David, he eagerly confesses. Nor does Giovanni's cramped, decrepit room belong to him, and, sadly, a good portion of the book takes place in the small, claustrophobic room that to David is almost as unbearable as the cell where the doomed Giovanni has a date with the guillotine after killing the owner of the bar where he used to work.

Hella, David's other lover, utters a line that must have had an abiding resonance for Baldwin: "Coming back to Paris . . . is always so lovely, no matter where you've been." And no doubt its appeal was even greater for a writer returning there after quick visits to Harlem. Later, she adds that Americans should never come to Europe, which rolls from her tongue like a cautionary tale for Baldwin, because "it means they can never be happy again." It is through an assortment of characters, and in this case none of them are black, that we realize the degree to which Baldwin is tormented by this dilemma. The blues of Paris obviously had a double meaning for Baldwin as he struggled to declare a homosexuality that, up to this time, had only been hinted at between the lines.

Both the spirit and name of Harlem resonate through "Sonny's Blues." First published in the *Partisan Review* in the summer of 1957, and later in the *Best American Short Stories* (1958) and *Going to Meet the Man* (1965), it's among

Baldwin's most anthologized stories. Harlem's influence on its residents is stated in the opening paragraphs when Sonny is remembered by his brother, the story's narrator, as wild but not crazy. "And he'd always been a good boy; he hadn't ever turned hard or evil or disrespectful, the way kids can, so quick, so quick, especially in Harlem," he wrote. The scenes here are unmistakably Harlem, and it's a Harlem accompanied by a variety of sounds, including spirituals, gospels, jazz, and the blues. The ever-present projects jut up out of the streets like "rocks in the middle of the sea." Sonny's brother, who is never named, laments that the stores and homes where they had come of age are no longer there. Gone are the basements where they first tried sex, gone were the rooftops from which they hurled cans and bricks.

Then, there's Harlem the trap: "Some escaped the trap, most didn't," the narrator says. "Those who got out always left something of themselves behind, as some animals amputate a leg and leave it in the trap. It might be said, perhaps, that I had escaped, after all, I was a school teacher; or that Sonny had, he hadn't lived in Harlem for years." At several junctures in the story the two brothers seem a composite of Baldwin, each at different times taking on aspects of his life. The narrator like Baldwin is the older brother, while Sonny, like Baldwin, has not lived in Harlem for several years. And each of them has an intimate understanding of the streets' hidden menace. To get out of Harlem, Sonny joined the army. The Harlem schools hadn't educated him and he was strung out on heroin. Sonny told his brother that he had to leave Harlem in order to get away from the drugs. But when he came back neither he nor the availability of drugs had changed.

Sonny's addiction and the brief discussion on the relationship between heroin and creativity come several pages after the mention of Charlie "Bird" Parker, who is one of Sonny's heroes, his avatar. Bird, one of the primary innovators of bebop jazz, had a genius that many of the jazz acolytes saw as indistinguishable from his addiction. At Minton's Playhouse on 118th Street, Bird and his "worthy constituents" had created music, a style, no less addictive than some of their habits. "Sometimes, you know, and it was actually when I was most out of the world, I felt that I was in it," he told his brother. This could be an expression applied equally to Sonny's feelings about Harlem.

What Baldwin had done for *Commentary* in 1948, he did for *Esquire* in 1960. As mentioned earlier, he wrote a searing description of Harlem in "Fifth Avenue, Uptown." Despite all the previous tirades about the insufferable living conditions in Harlem, there would be several more scathing indictments of his community and its unrelieved dinginess before he was through. At the end of the *Esquire* essay he remarked that to walk through the streets of Harlem is "to see what we, this nation, have become." A ghetto, he concluded, can be improved in one way only: "out of existence." We can assume that he meant ghetto as both a slum and a confined area.

Baldwin caused quite a furor when he described the Riverton Houses as "hideous" projects. His suggestion that the inhabitants of the projects urinated on the walls and generally defaced the units brought an angry response. A barrage of letters landed at *Esquire* magazine. "Baldwin, inexcusably had his facts wrong," wrote Julian Mayfield, who also had his facts wrong about the article appearing in *Holiday* magazine. "But what was of even greater interest was the basis on which he was attacked by outraged Harlem newspapers the following week. How dare he write such a thing about Riverton, where distinguished Negro judges, doctors and other professional people lived? One columnist hinted darkly, and somewhat in contradiction to the thesis of an impeccable community which he was defending, that the author would be well advised to remain downtown with his dilettante friends or, better, to return to Paris, as he would no longer be safe in the Harlem streets."

Baldwin fired back. "The inhabitants of Riverton were much embittered by this description; they have, apparently, forgotten how their project came into being; and have repeatedly informed me that I cannot possibly be referring to Riverton, but to another housing project which is directly across the street. It is quite clear, that I have no interest in accusing any individuals or families of the depredations herein described; but neither can I deny the evidence of my own eyes. Nor do I blame anyone in Harlem for making the best of a dreadful bargain. But anyone who lives in Harlem and imagines that he has not struck this bargain, or that what he takes to be his status (in whose eyes?) protects him against the common pain, demoralization, and danger, is simply self-deluded."

If Baldwin meant the housing units erected where he used to live at 2171 Fifth Avenue, then he was not talking about the Riverton houses that were built in 1948, where the family of Judge Bruce Wright lived. His son, state assemblyman Keith Wright, and his family continue to reside there. These units are mainly located from 135th Street to 138th Street. Baldwin's brother George noted the actual spot where they used to live, which is near the corner of 132nd Street. Those are the Lincoln Houses. To Baldwin's eyes, one high-rise housing complex was no different from another, no matter the class of its residents.

In the novel *Another Country*, published in 1962, Rufus Scott is a symbolic figure, and so long as he has a pulse, Harlem has a beat. But once he takes his life with a leap from the George Washington Bridge, Harlem—except the clubs where Scott's sister Ida performs—vanishes from Baldwin's third novel. And that *beat* explodes through an orchestra of instruments and body parts—tambourines, hands, feet, drums, pianos, laughter, curses, and razor blades. "The beat—in Harlem in the summertime one could almost see it, shaking above the pavements and the roof," Baldwin wrote. It is from this incessant, unsettling beat that Scott flees, but the flight is really from the "beat of his own heart."

The conglomeration of things that terrifies Rufus, Vivaldo, his friend, finds attractive. He is like a moth to the flame, facing the danger that looms at every turn because of his white skin. "He had felt more alive in Harlem, for he had moved in a blaze of rage and self-congratulation and sexual excitement, with danger, like a promise, waiting for him everywhere." For Vivaldo, Harlem is a battlefield where a keen instinct for survival is essential, where some "mother-wit" and ingenuity are necessary to negotiate safe passage both night and day. He knows that he is being watched with amusement and unkind contempt, that "he was just a poor white boy in trouble and it was not in the least original of him to come running to the niggers."

With Rufus no longer there to guide and chaperone him to and from the most dangerous liaisons, Vivaldo latches onto Rufus's sister, and Ida knows the byways and dark ways of Harlem as well as her brother, if not better. Small's Paradise is a favorite watering hole for Ida and crew, though it's a shame there isn't a more vivid rendering of its interior. (Baldwin had a major book party at the club, then owned by basketball great Wilt Chamberlain, when *Another Country* was published.) In short, when Rufus dies the "light went out" for Ida, Vivaldo, and several other characters, and for this reason, and possibly others, he is continuously discussed. "Why are we always talking about Rufus?" one of them asks disgustedly. The answer: there appears to be nothing else half as exciting or as provocative. No Rufus, no Harlem, no beat!

In *Another Country*, unlike in *Giovanni's Room*, Baldwin blends Harlem and Paris, essentially dividing the book between the two cities in a possible attempt to splice old-world Europe with the so-called new world and make "one society, a society realizing the intangible dreams of people." That intangibleness may also suffuse his fiction and nonfiction, that is, an attempt to see them as an unbroken continuum. Or, from another angle, his fiction allowed him the arena of expression unavailable in his nonfiction.

Numerous producers made overtures to Baldwin to give *Another Country* an afterlife in Hollywood, but, nothing happened. A deal with Tony Richardson appeared the most promising, but no major studio seemed interested.

Harlem may have been barely cited in the latter half of *Another Country*, but in his polemical essay *The Fire Next Time*, Baldwin again made the community a key focus. However, the content complemented the rhetorical flourish that enlivened the best of his previous screeds. Given that the first half of the book was addressed to his nephew, James, the recounting of his early years in Harlem made sense. Once more there is the young Baldwin fleeing to the church for protection and salvation. There is a recounting of his baptism; his standing in wonderment before the numerous street orators, possibly including Malcolm X; and most poignantly, a long account of his meeting Elijah Muhammad during a trip to Chicago. Harlem isn't necessary in this generic scenario of the "racial nightmare" that is part and parcel of the American experience.

Since *Blues for Mr. Charlie* was based on the Emmett Till murder, most of the action takes place in a southern town. Harlem is only mentioned in passing, though it comes alive in a passionate speech by Richard Henry, the play's victim. During an exchange with his grandmother, who admonishes him, telling him that he's going to be consumed by his hatred of white folks, he replies: "No I'm not . . . I'm going to make myself well with hatred." Hatred for Henry is not a poison, he declares. He promises to drink it gradually, a little each day and a "booster shot at night." "I'm going to keep it right here," he shouts, pointing to his head. "I'm going to remember Mama, Daddy's face . . . and Aunt Edna . . . and all those boys and girls of Harlem and all them pimps and whores and gangsters and all them cops. And I'm going to remember all the dope that's flowed through my veins . . . I'm going to remember all the jails I been in and the cops who beat me . . . I'm going to remember all that and I'll get well. I'll get well."

The Harlem of young Baldwin's life gushes forth at last in the novel *Tell Me How Long the Train's Been Gone*, which appeared to mixed reviews in 1968, just as many urban communities were revolting or on the verge of doing so. There's the contempt for the Jews who are the merchants or the landlords who make things miserable for the residents; there's the church and its tyrannical hold on his spirit; there are the demons of the street which keep him in perpetual flight and trepidation. Right away the images of Harlem are conjured: the barber and his big hands and "I thought of Harlem and all the needles I had seen there." He is possibly referring to the often swollen hands of intravenous drug users. There is also the fire escape, from where his dreams would soar and he can see a sweeping horizon with "windows flashing like signals in the sunlight."

That same sun is derided several pages later for what it reveals of the community's scars, and of the fact that "there was no joy." The protagonist, Leo Proudhammer, recalls the teasing and taunting he received as a child; the chants that he was a "sissy" were particularly distressful. There are at least two examples of characters, one black and one white, who had lived in Harlem. "Oh, that was a long time ago," explains a character that some biographers claim is based on Lee Strasberg, the renowned acting teacher. "It was suspected," Leo mused, "that the San Marquands [Saul and Lola] were Jewish, and people said terrible things about them behind their backs; but, on the other hand, they were friends with the stars of stage and screen. . . ." The bitterness between the character and the narrator has overtures of the charges of anti-Semitism Baldwin often had to endure. What seems to rile Leo is the man's condescending, "know-it-all-about-you-darkies" attitude. Leo's dislike for Saul is contrasted by his affection for Konstantine, a filmmaker who may have been modeled on Elia Kazan, one of Baldwin's dearest Jewish friends.

A scene in which Baldwin describes a few blocks along Morningside Avenue remarkably presages what is happening today in that part of Harlem and others as gentrification reconfigures the area. It is a neighborhood in transition; Lee sees that "white boys and black boys were in the streets, white girls and black girls, some carrying books." He walks down Madison Avenue, which "in no way resembles the American one." In an earlier essay Baldwin made a similar remark about Fifth Avenue.

The novel ends with Leo's father and his lover, Black Christopher, walking through the streets of Harlem, as if only on this turf could there be a possible resolution, as if this place most needed renewing by their combined strength of blackness.

In 1968, when *Tell Me How Long the Train's Been Gone* was published, Harlem, like many other urban communities in the world, was either simmering and waiting to explode or caught in the throes of civil upheaval. Without the creation and consolidation of the Studio Museum, the Schomburg Center, the National Black Theater, and other cultural groups, Harlem would have indeed gone up in smoke, long before the last passenger sought a seat on Baldwin's train. "Black Power," the catchphrase that first grabbed headlines after it was chanted by Stokely Carmichael in 1966 in Mississippi, was part of everyday speech in Harlem within months, and it was an expression that was by no means new to Baldwin. A year earlier when he had written a bristling response to allegations that he was anti-Semitic, he also wrote a favorable rejoinder to those who deplored Black Power. Toward the end of *Tell Me How Long*, it resonates in the attitude and behavior of Black Christopher, who is emblematic of black nationalism, and who would find his descendants and counterparts in *If Beale Street Could Talk*.

As we saw earlier, Baldwin was lambasted for chastising the projects in Harlem, and this dislike for the projects is a burden for Fonny, a main character in the novel *If Beale Street Could Talk*, which was an instant best seller in 1975. Through a first-person account that moves dynamically through his girlfriend's mind, Fonny, who is locked down in a New York City jail called the Tombs for a rape he didn't commit, detested the projects, cursing them for not providing enough space for him to work on his sculpture. The book's title is taken from an old blues song and has nothing at all to do with Memphis, though it may have been Baldwin's way of delivering a requiem to the slain Dr. King. When Tish, who is pregnant with Fonny's child, isn't visiting him in the Tombs, she's in Harlem with her family or in the Village, vainly seeking a way to get her man out of jail. It's not until after a couple of dozen pages that Harlem comes into the picture, and except for a couple of remarks, the scene could have been anywhere, which, again, may have been Baldwin's point. Here we discover that Fonny lives with his two sisters and his mother, who blame him for all of their misfortune.

But Baldwin doesn't cite the place as Harlem, nor is it named when Tish voices the limitations of her travel experience. "It's true that I haven't seen much of other cities, only Philadelphia and Albany," she complains, "but I swear New York must be the ugliest and the dirtiest city in the world. It must have the ugliest buildings and the nastiest people. It's got to have the worst cops. If any place is worse, it's got to be so close to hell that you can smell the people frying. And, come to think of it, that's exactly the smell of New York in the summertime." If there is any doubt she's really talking about Harlem, further on she gloats about her days at Abyssinian Baptist Church, and compared to the small, storefront, sanctified churches that Fonny attended, "it was brighter, and had a balcony."

This bit of Harlem, disgorged from Baldwin's memory of being a child and attending the church, is reminiscent of a community spirit, which in the early seventies was beginning to awaken from the punishing blight of the sixties. Perhaps this was the author's way of dealing with the lingering slumber, that is, Fonny's imprisonment was symbolic of Harlem's confinement and the slow pace of shaking off decades of urban decay. Or the lack of Harlem tapestry may have been the results of Baldwin's disconnect, his long separation, which forced him to consider it only in very general terms. Except for a few close-knit families, Harlem is a refuse, not a refuge for its bewildered denizens. In her review of the book, Joyce Carol Oates observed that blacks are constantly "at the mercy of whites" and "have not even the psychological benefit of the Black Power and other radical movements to sustain them."

Then again, knowing Baldwin's adopted role as a witness and a clarion, why shouldn't the cry of Tish's baby at the close of the novel be a wake-up call for a drowsy, apathetic Harlem?

A few weeks before the publication of *If Beale Street Could Talk*, Baldwin, as mentioned earlier, received the Centennial Medal for his accomplishments as an "Artist as Prophet" by the Cathedral of St. John the Divine, which is located at the borderline between Harlem and the Upper West Side. In the evening the shadows of the great church— the largest gothic cathedral in the world, larger than the combined size of Notre Dame and Chartres, and which Baldwin wrote about in "Stranger in the Village"–fall over Harlem, reaching up Amsterdam Avenue toward Columbia University. It was a scene like this, but a bit more somber, twelve years later when Baldwin's funeral was held in the church's enormous sanctuary. Now if the apses at St. John the Divine could talk–as they almost did during the funeral–what tales they would tell.

Just Above My Head (1979), Baldwin's last novel, includes several gripping tales, and of all his novels, is the one most solidly planted in Harlem. Hardly an aspect of Harlem is missed as he presents the vibrant, ever treacherous street life with gospel music forming the sound track to each chapter. The drugs that terrified him, the parties (particularly on Saturday nights), Sugar Hill, the Park Avenue railroad tracks where he grew up, the rock pile, the schools, the churches, including the Nation of Islam, the nightclubs, organizations, several institutions–all are vividly evoked. A gallery of Harlem notables are cited–Malcolm X, Dickie Wells, Harry Belafonte, and Father Divine–and like the multitude of bars, especially the legendary Red Rooster, located at 138th and Seventh Avenue, they give the book the deep textures of Harlem.

Much of this is viewed from the perspective of Hall Montana as he relates the adventurous life his brother, Arthur, has led. Their lives become even more intertwined when Hall begins to manage his brother's concert performances, presenting his great voice in theaters across the globe.

Ten years before *Just Above My Head* was published, the late Dr. Walter Turnbull founded the East Harlem Boy's Choir, at the Ephesus Seventh-Day Adventist Church. In the opening scenes of Book 3, "The Gospel Singer," Baldwin introduces Clarence Webster, a black music teacher who is an impresario, from Tennessee but operating out of Harlem. Webster has a striking resemblance to Turnbull, though he is ten years older than him. Both were born in the South (Turnbull in Greenville, Mississippi, in 1944) with a classical music background and are in charge of young men who have been rescued from the streets. When Webster suspects that two of his boys, Crunch and Arthur Montana, have begun a sexual relationship, he inquires but tells them "I'm an understanding guy." Whatever they are doing, he tells them, he "might want to do it too." What Webster suspects is true, but they keep him from getting involved. Still, to some extent Baldwin was prophetic because there were allegations of molestation surrounding Turnbull's Boys Choir of Harlem for years, and, though Turnbull was never charged, in 2004 one of his counselors was convicted of molesting one of the boys at the choir's academy. For failing to report the molestations, Turnbull and his brother were later forced to relinquish their control over the choir. Turnbull died in March 2007.

Interestingly, Arthur's perception of Webster in the North is different from the one he held while they were touring the South. "In Harlem," he muses, "Webster seems very sharp and hip, not old but not young. Here he has no age at all." If Harlem possesses the capability of altering how one is perceived, it can also take on a different aspect when seen by a former resident some years later. When Hall returns from fighting in Korea, and walks down the avenues of Harlem, it's as though he is seeing his old turf for the first time.

"We came into the sunlight, into the street. I had not seen these streets in so long, and I had seen so many things, that they hit me like a hammer. People adjust to the scale of things around them—cottages, streams, bridges, wells and narrow winding roads—and now I was in a howling wilderness, where everything was out of scale. For a moment I wondered how I could have lived here, how anyone could have lived here. I had not heard this noise in so long—incessant, meaningless, reducing everyone to a reflex, just as the towering walls of the buildings forced everyone to look down into the dog shit at their feet. No one ever looked up, that was certain, except to watch some maddened creature leap from the walls, or to calculate their own leap—yet people lived here, and so had I, and I would: what a wonder. What a marvel.

Hall confesses that he is both repelled and fascinated by Harlem, which is typical of Baldwin's ambivalence. Hall might be embittered, but he is home. And soon a phalanx of cops lets him know that the city's menace is always just around the corner, with a lethal billy club hovering just above his head. Even when Arthur, much later, is on tour in Paris, intimations of Harlem are inescapable. He is on the boulevard when a black man with a mustache and wearing a beret passes him swiftly in a "Harlem strut." One night, carousing in a crowded Parisian club, with a gaggle of women staring at him, he is once again, "insanely enough," reminded of Harlem. Toward the end of the book the scenes shift to midtown Manhattan and the Upper West Side. Harlem is given a final nod when Scott, the pianist, traveling with Arthur in the South, is not arrested but "kidnapped" for allegedly spitting on the sidewalk. Scott is loudmouthed and spunky and defiant of Dixie ways, and his Harlem attitude makes him a target of redneck sheriffs itching for an opportunity to put an uppity black boy in his place.

It took Baldwin three years to complete *Just Above My Head* and for much of that time, except for the last several months, he was in perpetual motion, running from one forum, lecture, party, bar, nightclub, rally, demonstration, or late-night drinking bout to another. That he was able to finish it at all is quite miraculous. Some of that helter-skelter activity put him back in touch with Harlem, and perhaps accounts for the freshly burnished memories of the community that abound in the novel. This was the last pass he would have at recalling and fictionally resurrecting his beloved Harlem. No matter where he chose to hide and to roam, Harlem was always his spiritual home, a place that was increasingly comfortable even as the danger intensified. "You don't ever leave home," he told a filmmaker, "you take it with you."

There is enough, at last, about the myth and mystery of Harlem in *Just Above My Head* to contest Albert Murray's notion that "he never really accounts for the tradition that supports Harlem's hard headed faith in democracy, its muscular Christianity, its cultural flexibility, nor does he account for its universally celebrated commitment to elegance in motion, to colorful speech idioms, to high style . . . Life in Harlem is the very stuff of romance and fiction, even as was life in Chaucer's England, Cervantes' Spain, Rabelais' France."

Baldwin rarely responded to critics about his work. He had produced his art and people could arrive at their own conclusions about its merits. But here are few samples of that art for Murray and others to consider. First from *Another Country*:

The beautiful children in the street black-blue, brown, and copper, all with a gray ash on their faces and legs from the cold wind, like the faint coating of frost on a window or a flower, didn't seem to care, that no one saw their beauty. Their elders, great, trudging, black women, lean shuffling men, had taught them, by precept or example, what it meant to care or not to care; whatever precepts were daily being lost, the examples remained, all up and down the street.

"Muscular Christianity" could describe this from *Go Tell It on the Mountain*:

On Sunday mornings the women all seemed patient, all the men seemed mighty. While John watched, the Power struck someone, a man or a woman; they cried out, a long wordless crying, and, arms outstretched like wings, they began the Shout. Someone moved a chair a little to give them room, the rhythm paused, the singing stopped, only the pounding feet and the clapping hands were heard; then another cry, another dancer; then the tambourines began again, like fire, or flood, or judgment. Then the church seemed to swell with the Power it held, and like a planet rocking in space, the temple rocked with the Power of God.

Romance warms *Just Above My Head*:

I lit a cigarette, and turned on my side, inhaling the memory of Ruth's odor, staring at the place her body had lain—I'm happy with her. Every inch of her body is a miracle for me; maybe because her body taught me so much about the miracle of my own. Sometimes, when I wake before she wakes, I lay as I lie now, and watch her: the square feet, which love walking the naked earth, the blunt stubborn, patient toes. And I kiss them. Kneeling, I kiss her legs, her thighs, my lips, my tongue, move upward to her sex, her belly button, her breasts, her neck, her lips, and I hold her in my arms, like some immense, unwieldy treasure. I, at least, thank God that I come out of the wilderness. My soul shouts hallelujah, and I do thank God.

Eight years after Murray had practically dismissed Baldwin, the two of them were part of a discussion with painter Romare Bearden and dancer Alvin Ailey in the living room of art publisher Hugh McKay. Reading the transcript of that meeting, one is struck by the cordialness between Baldwin and Murray; it's as though Baldwin either didn't remember the fury of Murray's dismissal or had chosen to let bygones be bygones. Rather than fume over the past, they reminisced about when they first met in Paris in the fifties and how they both came to grips with a different language and culture.

Baldwin's last paean to Harlem was published in *Essence* magazine in 1986. He had returned to his ancestral home for an event at the Apollo, a tribute to an old friend, drummer Art Blakey, whose enduring legacy was his leadership of the Jazz Messengers. What Baldwin saw as he surveyed his once "beautiful and organic community"—a rare description from him of his beloved Harlem—were neighborhoods on the cusp of gentrification. He noticed a high-rise taking shape on 123rd Street and assessed Harlem as a valuable piece of property where urban renewal was in the process of "gentrifying niggers out of it."

As ever, Baldwin was unable to suppress a paradox as he mulled over the situation, one that left him in distress but not despair. There was danger ahead for both black and white youths, he mused, and "each generation," he said, invoking that prophetic voice that was uniquely his, "has had to look out on this dangerous lonely place and try to invest it with coherence—*striving to make it my home.*" Home, however, was not the same anymore, and this was startlingly evident when he arrived in front of one of the places where he and his family used to live. "On the top floor of my building, 46 West 131st Street, between Fifth and Lenox Avenues, had been my father and my mother and my aunt, my brothers and my sisters, cousins, travelers, wonder, music, joy and I had witnesses!"

Returning to his hometown left Baldwin sad, and even the appearance of a few residents "from their caves," as he deemed it, had not sufficiently warmed him to the occasion. One could only wonder how these final impressions, this last look at his beginnings would be diffused in *The Welcome Table*, a play, and *Remember This House*, notes for his last novel. It's hard to say what creative twists and turns, what meandering thoughts would occur, but always, we can say with some certainty, he would be "*striving to make it my home.*"

Chapter 10

CRUSE'S CRISIS

Baldwin certainly had his share of detractors in Harlem, but none was as persistent as Harold Cruse, a pesky gadfly who published his most punishing critiques many years after their usefulness might have been most beneficial. Cruse's opening salvo seems to have been over Baldwin's first major essay, "The Harlem Ghetto," published in 1948. Years later, in 1963, Cruse composed "Negroes and Jews," an essay that was unpublished until the recent appearance of *The Essential Harold Cruse: A Reader*, edited by William Jelani Cobb. Cruse had begun his relentless, craven assault on Baldwin and his cohorts, including Paul Robeson, Lorraine Hansberry, John Oliver Killens, and Dr. John Henrik Clarke.

"The Harlem Ghetto," Cruse wrote, was really a "chic piece of magazine journalism that rehashed all the time-worn superficialities of Harlem 'local color' and decrepitude." If Baldwin had really wanted to play the "local color" card there were a number of sensational stories in Harlem he could have exploited, and one of the more bizarre ones occurred right in his old neighborhood on Fifth Avenue and 128th Street where the Collyer brothers had lived since 1909 and died in 1947. They were hermits who refused to throw anything away and within a few years, accumulated mountains of junk. Spooked by rumors that their home was the target of burglars, they built elaborate booby-traps. After one of the brothers went blind and died, the other brother was subsequently felled by his own booby-trap and pinned down by piles of rubbish. It was days before their bodies—mutilated by rats—were discovered. "We used to pass by their house all the time on the way to school," George Baldwin remembered. "Even then they were very strange since they were just about the only whites left in the neighborhood." A small, rubbish-free park stands today where the Collyers used to live.

Much of Cruse's criticism about the essay—its "glorified journalese"—would be rehashed, to use Cruse's word, several years later with the arrival of his monumental *The Crisis of the Negro Intellectual*. Cruse does not mention any of the supposedly time-worn articles with their "superficialities," but they certainly didn't come from him or from any of the pieces he submitted to the *Daily Worker* in the early fifties, where he was a part-time reviewer and librarian.

In his collection of essays *Rebellion or Revolution?* (1968), Cruse makes it clear that back in the late forties and fifties there was no craze for articles from black writers, which to some degree contradicts his statement above about time-worn articles about Harlem, especially if he means those possibly authored by black writers. In the same breath, he notes that his film and theater reviews were contemporaneous with Baldwin's first efforts, and thus equally ignored, as if to compare the mainstream *Commentary*, where Baldwin's essays appeared, with the Communist Party newspaper the *Daily Worker* where he was published. (For seven years he was a party member.)

In his discussion of "Negroes and Jews," Cruse uses Baldwin as his whipping boy, making his argument by scoring Baldwin as guest at a *Commentary* roundtable of Jewish intellectuals. Baldwin, Cruse asserted, was "bending over backward to avoid criticism of Jews while pretending to be angry with whites." This tactic, he continued, overlooked the fact that "if American Jews are 'caught in the American crossfire' they are also very much in control of the situation and have their enemies well 'cased' from all directions." Baldwin was not naïve to this power relationship; he used the forum as much as the Jewish intellectuals and magazines used him, and reviewing the debate during that roundtable, Baldwin was much more effective in his argument and remarks—holding his own against such formidable thinkers as Sidney Hook, Nathan Glazer, and Norman Podhoretz—than Cruse would ever allow.

A good example of Baldwin's effectiveness occurs toward the end of the debate in which he, literally and figuratively, gets the last word. "Mr. Baldwin," Podhoretz asks, "do you want to have the last word? Our time has almost run out, so it looks like you're going to get it whether you want it or not."

Baldwin pounced on the invitation, using the opening to further explain what he meant by a radical transformation of society: "I have in mind several very concrete things . . . that if one really intends to eliminate ghettos, one has to be prepared to deal with banks, the real estate boards, and all the other groups and pressures which in fact create ghettos and keep children in prison. To deal with these power groups is obviously to undertake a radical transformation." Baldwin agreed with Gunnar Myrdal, the great Swedish social scientist, that black Americans were not the only submerged and oppressed people in the nation, but "my hope is this," he added "and I think it is only hope: that when *all* the submerged, when *all* the oppressed, when all the penalized, and when *all* the subjugated are finally liberated, then we too will be liberated by the new energy that will be released into the mainstream of American society." If this sounds like someone knuckling under, or in awe of, or intimidated by white intellectuals, then Cruse was just incapable of objectively evaluating Baldwin's prowess.

Who was Harold Cruse? Here's how he described himself: "As a boy I attended three kinds of educational institutions—the completely integrated schools of suburban Queens, the predominantly black Harlem schools, and the segregated all-black schools of Virginia." Cruse, who died in the spring of 2005, was born in Petersburg, Virginia, in 1916. His father, then divorced from his mother, brought Cruse to New York to live with him. From his early years, there was the urgency to write, much of which was inspired by accompanying his father to the theater and to vaudeville performances, where he was immersed in the song, dance, and theater of the 1920s and 1930s. After a military stint, he returned to his beloved Harlem and quickly resumed his inconspicuous presence at rallies and clubs. "I spent the years from 1945 to about 1952 wrestling with this perplexity (understanding what had happened during the previous generation)," he wrote, "and trying to understand why I was such a glaring intellectual misfit—an incomprehensible gadfly to some, and a pretentious neophyte to others, those whose politics I criticized."

Gadfly and *misfit* are the operative words here, because rather than actively engage in the heated intellectual and political debates of the period, he was more comfortable and content to keep his opinions to himself. He began writing reviews for various left publications but had no idea where he was headed, politically or from a literary point of view. "I came through it all badly mauled, scarred, traduced, defeated in a score of battles, but determined to win that war even if that required becoming a critical Kamikaze fighter on the cultural front." Without any lengthy formal education, Cruse took to the streets, where he gathered his lessons on the "avenues of academics," listening to the likes of Hubert Harrison, W. A. Domingo, Claudia Jones, Cyril Briggs, Grace Campbell, and Harry Haywood. Later, he would accuse a coterie of other scholars and researchers as being autodidacts but it is a title that rightly belonged on his resume as well.

By the early sixties, Cruse felt he had arrived at a "definitive critical construct," and within a few years this ensemble of ideas, albeit burdened with contradictions and questionable logic, were the wellspring of *The Crisis of the Negro Intellectual*. The book arrived at a time when black social and political thought was caught in a maelstrom of public discourse, driven mainly by the argument between "narrow nationalists and mechanical Marxists." Cruse entered the fray, offering an extensive exegesis on everything from Black Nationalism, blacks in the Communist Party, significant West Indian leaders, and the role of black intellectuals, and all of this was conducted for the most part through a prism of cultural activity, organizations, and institutions in Harlem. And at the core of his philosophy was the notion that it was possible to reason with racism via art, a strategy that was essential to the artists of the Harlem Renaissance. Both the content and the size of the book were intimidating.

Cruse was quickly the lightning rod among black public intellectuals and subsequently there were contending forces: those who championed his conclusions versus those who, like Dr. John Henrik Clarke, believed Cruse had raised a number of important questions "but provided very few answers." Of course, Dr. Clarke would stand opposed to much of what Cruse proposed since he was among those Cruse took to task by insisting they had fallen far short of delivering the critical leadership the black community so desperately needed. And the issue of leadership is the source of much of the derision Cruse created. Even if Dr. Clarke, Hansberry, Killens, Robeson, and Baldwin were artists with no intention of being "race leaders," Cruse held them accountable, and in fact concluded they had failed in their mission. It seems rather peculiar that a writer, painter, dancer, actor, or singer, none of whom are elected officials or even at the head of an organization, can be deemed to have neglected his or her "obligation" to lead the people. In other words, if we follow this half-baked logic, the plumber is berated for being an incompetent electrician; the filmmaker, alas, is without worth for not having led his people into the Promised Land. Because a gifted musician does not possess the skill or wherewithal to deliver a rousing political speech, Cruse is ready to curse him, to assign him to the purgatory of failed race leaders.

Baldwin never aspired to be a race leader, so it seems grossly unfair to suggest that he was less than adequate as a

savior of his race. To be sure, most of Baldwin's books were
infused with the hope of uplifting black Americans and
others, but this intent cannot be compared to the promises of
an elected official who for some reason abdicated his responsibility.

Having charged Baldwin with being a spokesman for his
race, Cruse then ties him to the mast and lashes him. Cruse
states that Baldwin, as such a spokesperson, allowed himself
to be trapped "by the pundits who understand political and
philosophical polemics much better than he." By the very fact
that Baldwin is a black artist, he is not conditioned by the
same exigencies facing the white artist. He cannot be, Cruse
says, above race, caste, and class, particularly if he has
declared himself a voice for his oppressed people. Unlike the
white artist, who has the option to either escape or to obscure
reality, Baldwin, as the "spokesman" for his race, has no such
option; he must deliver the message. But Cruse concludes
Baldwin dropped the ball entirely. "The significance of his
message has begun to pale in inverse ratio to the increase of
his polemic passion," Cruse wrote in "James Baldwin, the
Theater and His Critics," an unpublished essay in 1963. All
of this sounds pretty impressive and possibly true, if in fact
Baldwin had actually taken the role as spokesman for his
race, an assignment he neither sought nor assumed. "It's like
Sidney Poitier being America's only Negro movie star," Baldwin told Nat Hentoff of the *New York Herald Tribune* as he
indirectly addressed Cruse's gripe. "That's the country's fault,
not ours. But I'm still trying to speak just for me, not for
twenty million people." Twenty years later, during an interview with a reporter, Baldwin expressed his position even
more explicitly. "I don't consider myself a spokesman—I have

always thought it would be rather presumptuous . . . Once I was in the civil rights milieu, once I'd met Martin Luther King, Jr. and Malcolm X and Medgar Evers and all those other people, the role I had to play was confirmed. I didn't think of myself as a public speaker, or as a spokesman, but I knew I could get a story past the editor's desk."

A spokesman, as Henry Louis Gates, Jr. has explained, must have a grasp of his role and an unambiguous message to deliver. "Baldwin had neither, and when this was discovered a few short years later, he was relieved of his duties, shunted aside as an elder, and retired, statesman." The irony, Gates continued—and it is quite consistent with that tincture of paradox that permeated Baldwin's life—is that "he may never fully have recovered from the demotion from a status he had always disavowed."

But it is not only Baldwin's so-called role as spokesperson that perturbs Cruse; it's his play *Blues for Mr. Charlie*, which Cruse contends is a "throwback to the social realism of the 1930s." And one wonders what's so terribly offensive about that? Some of the finest plays of the American stage, productions such as *Waiting for Lefty*, *Awake and Sing!*, and *Golden Boy*—all by Clifford Odets—were exemplars of social realism, a genre that in the hands of Wright, whom Baldwin assailed, "was consistent with his Marxist beliefs and sense of the reality and brutality of black life," Margaret Walker concluded. Baldwin made it explicitly clear that his play was based on the murder of Emmett Till, a youth who went to Mississippi in the summer of 1955 to visit relatives and was brutally killed by two white men after they learned he had whistled at Carolyn Bryant, the wife of one of the men. And since it is based on Till's victimization, it would not be accurate to suggest, as Cruse does, that the victim should have taken some action. Till, like the play's victim, Richard Henry, is a helpless target, and after Henry gives his gun to his father, he is equally defenseless. Yes, Baldwin gives him a weapon, but Henry feels it is more dutiful to turn the gun over to his father and thereby honor his father's nonviolent philosophy. Moreover, to have kept the gun would have contradicted the reality of Till's situation. For Cruse to suggest, almost categorically, that Baldwin does not believe in arms is to ignore the potential use of the gun in the hands of Reverend Henry. He has it under the pulpit, next to his Bible.

For Cruse, Baldwin's message is one of "racial doom," given the symbolic death of Richard Henry. But the ending of the play, with Parnell asking to join Reverend Henry and his followers in a march for equal rights—as well as Reverend Henry's new choice of using his son's gun instead of "turning the other cheek" of the New Testament—portends tactics beyond nonviolence, which, historically, would be quite fitting since Baldwin would soon be enamored with the Black Panther Party and the righteous fulminations of Robert Williams, whose book *Negroes with Guns* revived an old militancy in black America. Cruse seems disturbed that Baldwin has offered Henry up like a sacrificial lamb on the "altar of hate." But this too is consistent with the notion that Till was a kind of sacrificial lamb and his death inspired the slowly emerging civil rights movement. "I believe my son was sent for that purpose," said Till's mother, Mamie Till Mobley. "And I don't think he died in vain."

Baldwin's character Parnell James is in many ways representative of the white liberal caught between the polarities of allegiance: an unbroken loyalty to his white friends and relatives, most of whom are unadulterated racists and segregationists, or stepping across the racial divide in unity with the blacks of his small town and so being banished forever. Literary critic Daryl Dance argues correctly that Cruse misinterprets James's behavior and at the same time muddles Baldwin's take on liberalism. Dance says that Cruse "comments at some length about Baldwin's failure to defend adequately and substantiate his attack on white liberals, suggesting in a footnote that Parnell James is 'so sympathetically portrayed as to border on the maudlin, despite the author's professed view of white liberals,' an accusation that arises from a faulty reading of the play, since Parnell represents the weakness, ineffectiveness, and unreliability of the liberal."

Liberalism would be a main theme in Cruse's magnum opus, and therein Baldwin is the ringleader of the black intellectuals that Cruse skewers. A year after the above unpublished essay, Cruse renewed his attack on Baldwin, chastising him for being less than prepared to deal with the issue of "sociology and the economics jazz" during a debate with white liberals, the roundtable discussion addressed earlier in this chapter. "This failure to discuss the racial conflicts either in terms of possible practical solutions, or in terms of American economic and sociological realities, made Baldwin's assault on white liberals a futile rhetorical exercise; it was further weakened by the intellectual inconsistencies, incoherence and emotionalism of his line of argument." A cursory review of that debate shows that Baldwin fared pretty well and it is to his favor that he admitted that he wasn't prepared to discuss, in any great detail, matters for which he felt inadequate and unqualified, something that Cruse seemed unable to do on any subject or issue.

The attack on Baldwin that Cruse had begun in 1963 (or possibly earlier in the pages of *Studies on the Left*) gained more intensity three years later when he accused Baldwin of writing as though there was no such thing "as a distinct middle class that is setting the tone and pace of the Negro movement." Baldwin constantly praised the courageous commitment of all the civil and human rights leaders, with special accolades for Dr. King, Medgar Evers, and Malcolm X, all of whom were decidedly ensconced in the black middle class or considered among the "race leaders." Baldwin even saw in them nobility, noting the sacrifices they made to a movement that often led them to forsake their families. The recognition Baldwin gave to students, many of them products of the black middle class, especially those at Howard University, for their unflinching commitment to SNCC and other organizations is evidence that he knew exactly where the civil rights engine was and the significant role of the students. It is somewhat ironic that Cruse would lambaste Baldwin for not knowing of the pivotal role of the black middle class in the civil rights movement and then punish Langston Hughes for failing to "criticize the black middle class bourgeoisie." Damned if you do and damned if you don't.

Cruse, or his editors, was even guilty of putting controversial words in Baldwin's mouth without offering any attribution. In his chapter on Paul Robeson in *The Crisis of the Negro Intellectual,* Cruse includes a quote allegedly from Baldwin. But, he provides no footnote: "It is personally painful to me to realize that so gifted a man as Robeson should have been tricked by his own bitterness and by a total inability to understand the nature of political power in general, or Communist aims in particular, into missing the point of his own critique, which is worth a great deal of thought." If Baldwin indeed possessed these reservations about Robeson, which Cruse fails to substantiate, by 1977 his views of the great activist had changed dramatically. In an article in the *Black Collegian* in 1998, Paul Robeson, Jr. wrote that his father's "nobility stemmed from his internalization of these values [sacrificing for what you know is right, fighting for the downtrodden] and the clarity of his inner vision enabled him to personify images of strength and dignity with a universal appeal. The late James Baldwin alluded to Paul Robeson's historic cultural stature and his symbolic meaning to the younger generations in . . . [an] eloquent passage of an open letter written in 1977 on behalf of a group of Black notables who were protesting against a Broadway play titled *Paul Robeson* which, they felt, trivialized Robeson's life and misrepresented his character." Even earlier, in a *Freedomways* magazine salute to Robeson in 1965 at the Hotel Americana, chaired by Ossie Davis and Ruby Dee, Baldwin proclaimed his support for Robeson. In his remarks he noted that "in the days when it seemed that there was no possibility in raising the individual voice and no possibility of applying the rigors of conscience, Paul Robeson spoke in a great voice which creates a man." Another firebrand, Bobby Seale, a founder of the Black Panther Party, had also earned a spot on Baldwin's busy schedule when the writer penned a foreword to Seale's second autobiography, *A Lonely Rage,* in October 1977. "I did not go through what Bobby, and his generation, went through," he wrote. "The time of my youth was entirely different and the savage irony of hindsight allows me to suggest that the time of my youth was far less hopeful."

In 1978, Baldwin, still on the ramparts against the depiction of Robeson by James Earl Jones that was readied for Broadway, told an audience at Hunter College: "The popular culture has to find a way to make Robeson moving, charming, noble and innocent, and above all irrelevant." At least the last objective fits well with Cruse's obsession to denounce Robeson and Baldwin at every turn.

None of Cruse's comments on Robeson was as woefully wrong as his decision to select Robeson as symptomatic of the "Negro-actor-performer-singer" ambivalent communion with the "Negro creative artist upon whom the interpreters seldom depend for their artistic accomplishments or financial status." Cruse's suggestion that Robeson as an interpretative artist limited or excluded his creativity is ridiculous. Many theatergoers recall how Robeson, offended by some of the lyrics in "Ol' Man River," changed lines in order to remove racial epithets. Cruse should have also been aware that Robeson was deeply steeped in the black cultural heritage from which he drew some of his most memorable performances. "For the first five years as a singer," Robeson observed in his autobiography, "my repertoire consisted entirely of my people's songs." Robeson could have added that he was the first concert singer to present a program comprised mainly of songs composed and arranged by African Americans.

Cruse's attempt to drive a wedge between Robeson and Baldwin failed, but undaunted, the gadfly tried another ploy, this time pouncing on writer Julian Mayfield, who had defended Baldwin in his essay "And Then Came Baldwin" by lamenting: "Would that the artist could be a scholar and vice versa, but he rarely is." The old adage about the friend of my enemy is my enemy applies in this instance and Cruse is a relentless hound on Mayfield's tail. The blindness he attributed to Baldwin's inability to see that the "Negro movement" was a product of the middle class was now a liability for Mayfield. "He saw the new Negro movement as a challenge to traditional middle class leadership without understanding that it too was, with few exceptions, also strongly middle class oriented," Cruse posited. The logic of Cruse's argument might be applicable if it's possible to suspend disbelief that Mayfield vis-à-vis Baldwin is basically politically naïve, but the improbability of this is manifest in their sophisticated and often complex essays to the contrary. "At any rate, Baldwin is neither an historian, economist nor a political scientist, but a creative writer whose work testifies that his layman's knowledge of these fields is not as shallow as his critics suggest," Mayfield wrote in the same essay cited above, and what he says of Baldwin is applicable to him as well.

"If Mayfield's words failed to forge a consensus in the black community regarding Baldwin's stature," wrote Peniel Joseph in his lively and immensely informative study of Black Power, "they illustrated the breadth of his appeal."

One of the more perplexing, if not baffling assertions by Cruse is that Baldwin's voice is a "timorous" one, that he and his cohorts in the civil rights movement are "frightened by the temper of the times." They may have been, to some degree, frightened—and who wouldn't be, going unarmed against the violent menace of the KKK and other arch-segregationists. But they nonetheless did not shy away from the battlegrounds of the South. And where was Cruse during these dangerous, perilous times? About the closest he came to the actual turmoil in the South was via a newsreel, or hovering in the background at a press conference called by a member of the civil rights movement, fresh from some near-death experience.

Amiri Baraka (LeRoi Jones) is the next on Cruse's hit list, and as expected Cruse associates him with Baldwin and the "white-Negro-Jewish" consortium. But to make this amalgam work, it is necessary that their attitudes toward Jews be opposite sides of the same coin. Jones and other artists, such as musician Archie Shepp, are, from Cruse's perspective, "the reverse side of James Baldwin's superficialities on Negro-Jewish relations. Baldwin refuses to 'hate' Jews on ethical grounds; both Jones and Shepp refused to 'love' Jews on some other ethical grounds." Once more we are faced with a neat bit of sophistry in which Cruse tangles the reader in a tautology. Perhaps more than anything, Baldwin is tarred with the same brush Cruse lavishes on Jones and Shepp, whom he defines as "artists who function in cultural and artistic spheres without being motivated by a serious, well-thought-out literary and cultural critique on the white society they are attacking." It is safe to assume that he meant the same indictment for Baldwin.

Cruse was able to gather all his opponents in one baleful hook when Baldwin and his coterie, notably Clarke, Killens, Ossie Davis, Ruby Dee, and Alice Childress gathered for a conference at the New School for Social Research in New York City in 1965. (Two years earlier, after the four girls in Birmingham were killed when their church was bombed, this same group, including Odetta and Louis Lomax, rented New York's Town Hall and demanded that Christmas be declared a day of mourning.) And Cruse must have leaped for joy upon reading a notice in the *New York Times* about the event in which Baldwin was called a "literary prostitute." The conference also gave Cruse an opportunity to stir up a little mischief between Clarke and Baldwin, selecting a quote from Clarke where he was mainly chiding Ralph Ellison for his absence from the political scene. Clarke told the forum, referring to the decade following Ellison's completion of *Invisible Man*, that the author "had been in flight" from his people, much like Baldwin, but at least Baldwin "did come back and enter the mainstream of the struggle. Whether he is psychologically back home completely opens maybe (another) question. But at least he knows the road that leads to home. But Mr. Ralph Ellison seems to have been going further away from home in that sense." In 1993, in the preface to a reprint of *Harlem Voices*, which he edited, Clarke extolled the deceased Baldwin's "brilliant career that lasted for more than a generation." Clarke may have smoothed things with Baldwin in the years before his death, but Cruse wasn't through with Clarke, charging that since he was not a creative writer he was in no position to criticize Ellison's work. Again Cruse was wrong. Clarke was a poet and short story writer of considerable skill, and his story "The Boy Who Painted Christ Black" has been anthologized in numbers vastly exceeding even one production of a Cruse play.

While Cruse was greatly appreciated by the Afrocentric school of thought—and Molefi Asante was a chief flag waver, praising Cruse for reinvigorating cultural nationalism with his anti-Marxist analysis—there were others who were less than enthusiastic about Cruse's conclusions. It seems rather contradictory that Cruse can be seen as someone who reinvigorates a culture when he worked so diligently to destroy some of the primary forces in African American culture. William Jelani Cobb, in a very thoughtful introduction to *The Essential Harold Cruse*, has rounded up some of the naysayers. Noted Caribbean authority Winston James found Cruse's book to be anti-Caribbean and "mired in a subjective response that undermines its own authority," Cobb wrote, but it's a passionate subjectivity which may be the element that has given the book enduring cachet. It's also a subjectivity that relies far too much on inaccuracy and polemical zeal, James argues. At last the book, he asserts, is "long, rambling and cantankerous" and, more grievously, "the analysis itself is flawed and the research upon which is it based is uneven, inadequate, partial, distorted, too feeble to carry the heavy load of Cruse's many and controversial judgments." As Dr. John Henrik Clarke said of Cruse, and James agrees, Cruse was good at raising good questions, but he was unable to sufficiently answer hardly any of them. Jerry Gafio Watts, according to Cobb, felt Cruse was in error for relying on the axis of nationalism and integrationism that "underestimated the degree to which the most vehement black nationalist intellectual was fundamentally American."

Cruse has even been taken to task by feminist scholars Beverly Guy-Sheftall and Michele Wallace. Guy-Sheftall voices her disappointment at the invisibility of black women intellectuals "except for Lorraine Hansberry, who is mostly vilified . . . in his profoundly patriarchal text." Of course, Cruse cannot by any stretch of the imagination have been alone in this bias since, save for a Margaret Walker here and a Claudia Jones there, one is hard-pressed to list more than a handful of prominent black female intellectuals during this era.

And like Watts, Guy-Sheftall feels that Cruse's overarching paradigm of viewing black progress through the lens of integration and nationalism is "overly simplistic." Wallace, on the other hand, chides Cruse for missing the implications of his own scholarship: "'Integration,' he warned, 'is leading to cultural negation.' As Cruse saw it, integration-minded intellectuals like James Baldwin and Lorraine Hansberry were infected with a lethal dose of false consciousness—a severe case of neither knowing nor caring what was *really* black."

To be really black—and Wallace raises an interesting point—would be akin to adopting an almost pure form of Pan-African thought that would not allow any concession or consolation for Eurocentricism. Such rigid guidelines would negate both Baldwin and Cruse, or, in a perverse way, place them in the same camp as Jacob Carruthers does in *Intellectual Warfare*. Carruthers states that Pan-African Nationalism is inimical to the European intellectual tradition, and is a direct threat to its very existence. He makes this point while eviscerating the ideas of Cornel West and his attempt to balance Pan-African and European ideas. "This African challenge offends European scholars and makes them uncomfortable," Carruthers wrote. West, however, is not alone in his far-fetched desire to meld the two streams of thought, Carruthers continues. "Other African intellectuals who tried and failed in this regard include W.E.B. Du Bois, Richard Wright, Chester Himes, Ralph Ellison, James Baldwin and Harold Cruse." No doubt Baldwin and Cruse would be amused to find themselves placed within the same construct of inability.

This failure, put another way by culturologist Greg Tate in his summary of Crusian analysis, meant that the intellectuals found it difficult to fuse agendas of "protest and reform politics with self-help economics, sophisticated cultural critiques, and a Marxian take on the political economy of capitalism." Imagine a discussion where Elijah Muhammad, Dr. Frances Cress Welsing, Ivan Van Sertima, and Angela Davis are deliberating the significance of the race/class dichotomy (as to which was the principal contradiction) and you have some indication of the challenge of forging ties between fairly disparate worldviews. Baldwin and Cruse looked at black and white reality through different prisms, were bothered by separate fears, and possessed unique visions about change and possibility. There was wiggle room, conceptual space in Baldwin's universe for white comrades, but for Cruse white allies were anathema, and eventually would betray the once-agreed-upon mission. The two men's disagreements about things, then, were inevitable, and while they both admitted flaws in their outlook and propositions, their weaknesses were different and without any common ground.

If Cruse could have accepted the notion that Baldwin, in a very strict sense, was not part of the so-called Harlem left-wing literary and cultural elite, many of whom sanctioned the rejection of Cruse's art and politics, he might have spared him as he set out to revisit those ghosts of the forties where sectarian rivalry marked his passage. For the most part, Baldwin steered clear of the left, but nonetheless ran right into Cruse who, in an obviously undisguised way, was seeking the very tangible successes Baldwin had achieved.

Chapter 11

Baraka

The assassination of Malcolm X in 1965 weighed heavily on Baldwin, and to balance his tenuous emotional state he headed to the South. He linked arms with James Forman and folk singer Joan Baez in the third, more successful march from Selma to Montgomery. It would prove to be a tragic yet momentous stage of the civil rights movement.

About the same time LeRoi Jones, not yet an Imamu, Ameer, or Amiri Baraka, headed north to Harlem, looking for political stability beyond his total immersion in the white life of Greenwich Village. In his autobiography, he compared this new phase as a transition summed up in the works of Frantz Fanon, Amilcar Cabral, and Aimé Césaire, with a special emphasis on the Martinican's *Notebook of a Return to the Native Land (Cahier d'un retour au pays natal)*. "The middle class native intellectual, having outintegrated the most integrated, now plunges headlong back into what he perceives as blackest, native-est," he confessed. "Having dug, finally, how white he has become, now, classically, comes to

his countrymen charged up with the desire to be black . . . a
fanatical patriot!"

An energetic Jones and his potent posse wasted no time
sparking the incipient Black Arts Movement, and within
weeks they were roughly allied with the then nascent
HARYOU-ACT (Harlem Youth Opportunities Unlimited–
Associated Community Teams) programs, established ostensibly to ward off what many public officials predicted was
going to be a long hot summer of protest and political dis-
content. The sprigs of black cultural nationalism flowered in
wild fantastic fashion, and Jones's poems, plays, and charisma were at the center, though he admitted he wasn't
exactly sure what was going on since he was caught in the
eye of this artistic hurricane. "I had no formal definition of
cultural nationalism," he wrote. "I didn't even correctly know
what it was. But certainly, it was all around us then, the
Nation of Islam the most known. But Malcolm's death ended
any would-be hookup with the Nation for me and most of
my friends."

Curiously, Jones, then a rather committed nationalist long
before his conversion to Marxism, was often at odds with
Harlem's radical fringe, most notably Bill Epton of the Progressive Labor Party, which would play such a decisive role
in the struggle to free the Harlem Six. But this was the least
of Jones's problems—there was dissension in his own ranks,
and his temporary venture into polygamy only exacerbated
the growing tension. "Our politics," he stated, "first and ultimately, was the reason the program and its development
were in such disorder; our politics which flowed from our
mix-matched and eclectic ideology. We had straight-out
white supremacy bourgeois opinions mixed with mass felt

revolutionary ones. We wanted to destroy the system and
didn't realize that we still carried a great deal of that system
around with us behind our eyes."

With things in complete disarray, his personal life in a
shambles, and his one most trusted comrade, Larry Neal,
shot in the leg, Jones felt it was time to get back to Newark,
his hometown. The adventure in Harlem had lasted less than
a year, but his reputation as a writer had reached well beyond
that community. In fact, the brief tenure in Harlem had only
interrupted his critique against Baldwin, which began two
years earlier when he paired Baldwin with South African
writer Peter Abrahams, both of whom he charged with being
overly concerned with the "individual." This is odd since a
more communal outlook—the good of the group before the
good of the one—was not part of Jones's worldview either at
that time. Moreover, Jones claimed that Abrahams and Baldwin were able "to shriek the shriek of a fashionable international body of white middle class society," and this gave them
all the pretense of a "Joan of Arc of the cocktail party" that
"is being presented through the writings and postures of men
like these."

Among the more egregious accusations from Jones about
the two writers was that they, "want to live free from such
'ugly' things as 'the racial struggle' because (they imply) they
simply cannot stand what it does to men." To condemn Baldwin in this way is to ignore that by this time he had already
written six books, including *The Fire Next Time*. So it seems,
on the face of it, quite ludicrous to suggest that he was less
inclined to be part of the "struggle." Jones went so far as to
assert that if Baldwin and Abrahams turned white there
would be no more noise from them. With them having their

"wish" to turn white, Jones continued, "perhaps the rest of us can get down to the work at hand. Cutting throats!"

From this jeremiad it is easy to chart Jones's steady absorption of black nationalism that would become even more creative and lyrical by the time he arrived in Harlem for a reprise. And inasmuch as he had been confined to whiteness by Jones, the following poem certainly applied to Baldwin:

> *We are unfair, and unfair*
> *We are black magicians, black arts*
> *we make in black labs of the heart.*

> *The fair are*
> *Fair, and death*
> *ly white.*

> *The day will not save them*
> *and we own*
> *the night.*

Jones's distance from Baldwin during this period might have been aided by Jones's association with Harold Cruse. Cruse taught black history under Jones's jurisdiction at the Black Arts and Repertory Theater and School (a venture Cruse would later disparage) and there must have been moments when they shared their common dislike of Baldwin and his literary ascendance. After Jones split from Harlem— or was run out of Harlem according to some who were there— he returned, as I have said, to Newark, where he was born, and started another black arts organization. At the opening ceremony, Jones observed, was Stokely Carmichael and

Cruse. But the restless Jones refused to allow any grass to grow under his feet and in quick succession he had forged an alliance with Maulana Karenga and adopted the Kawaida theory or philosophy as his doctrine and way of life. In effect, they were joined by their "slave names." Ron Everett was now in cahoots with Everett Jones. For a while they were extremely compatible but soon Jones would be anointed Ameer Barakat and then Amiri Baraka and an orthodox Sunni Muslim. Only Amina, his wife, and her regard for the class and gender question, curtailed him from sinking irretrievably into the nationalism of Spirit House, the Black Arts Movement, and the Congress of African People.

Then came the storm of disinformation from the FBI's counterintelligence program (COINTELPRO), which put the various militants at one another's throats. "I had tried to organize a national united front structure with US [Karenga's group], RAM [Revolutionary Action Movement], SNCC [Student Nonviolent Coordinating Committee], RNA [Republic of New Afrika], and the Panthers," Baraka related in his autobiography, which in far too many ways is unreliable. "Eldridge [Cleaver] talked bad about the idea over the phone. More and more the Panthers began to denounce the 'porkchop nationalists'—obvious Cleaver terminology—and more and more Karenga's people called the Panthers 'kamikaze niggers.' It is proven now from Freedom of Information Act files that the FBI orchestrated much of this discord between the two organizations."

Neither Baldwin nor Baraka was aware that both had been under surveillance by the FBI ever since their association with the Fair Play for Cuba Committee in 1960. Although Baldwin was a listed sponsor of the organization—

and there were a number of leftist organizations that had used his name—he did not travel with the group when it was invited to Cuba. The committee, founded by Vincent T. Lee in 1960, was among the leading organizations of leftists demanding a policy of "hands off of Cuba." It was made infamous when Lee Harvey Oswald opened a branch in New Orleans. (He subsequently composed a flier demanding that the United States keep its hands off Cuba and soliciting members to the organization. No one joined his branch, though he did send out honorary memberships to several notable activists. In the winter of 1963, shortly after the assassination of President Kennedy, the New Orleans office was closed.)

Baraka (then Jones) wrote a long detailed account of the Cuba trip and the cadre he traveled with, including Cruse, Dr. John Henrik Clarke, Robert Williams, who would later seek exile in Cuba, painter Ed Clarke, and Julian Mayfield. "There were twelve of us scheduled to go to Habana, July 20," Jones wrote (there is also an account of this trip by Harold Cruse in *The Crisis of the Negro Intellectual*). "Twelve did go, but most were last-minute replacements for those originally named. James Baldwin, John Killens, Alice Childress, Langston Hughes, were four who were replaced." Even in Cuba, Jones found it necessary to conjure Baldwin. One day at a bar he ran into a Cuban who wanted Jones to tell him all about Harlem. Jones said that was the wildest thing he had heard that night and he asked his inquisitor: "What's the matter, didn't you read Jimmy Baldwin's article in *Esquire*?" The man had no idea what Jones was talking about and to relieve him from a frozen, quizzical state, Jones gave him a short history of Harlem.

The article Jones was referring to was Baldwin's essay "Fifth Avenue, Uptown." Jones does not say exactly what he told the Cuban but if he had quoted Baldwin's article with any accuracy the listener would have heard of a Harlem that was hardly better than Habana, and a Harlem that was on the verge of explosion with the ever-swelling Puerto Rican population. Between 1910 and 1945, the Puerto Rican community in the city had increased from 1,600 to 135,000. And this number had mushroomed to more than 600,000 by the mid-sixties.

There may have been just a bit of gruff from Jones about Baldwin and his article of July 1960, but the two were on the same page by April 1968. They, along with Norman Mailer, were among several well-known writers who signed a letter protesting the murder of Black Panther Party member Little Bobby Hutton in Oakland, California. Hutton, the first to join the party, had surrendered to the police following a shoot-out, but was brutally gunned down by the police with his arms raised in the air. Eldridge Cleaver was also in the shoot-out, but was apparently viewed as less threatening when he emerged from the smoke-filled house stark naked.

In 1974, Baraka made another sudden ideological shift, now to the left, sending many of his followers hurtling forward, bothered and bewildered. While Baraka was constantly on the move politically, Baldwin was on the move, period, traveling back and forth from his home in France and on a book tour promoting *If Beale Street Could Talk*. By the summer Baldwin was back in France just in time to celebrate his fiftieth birthday. Baraka and his wife were by now either en route to or enjoying themselves in Somalia, where it dawned on them that their struggle for total liberation had always been right under their nose.

A decade later, in 1984, Baraka was again berating Baldwin in an essay titled "The Revolutionary Tradition in Afro-American Literature" and, of course, Baldwin is not included in the revolutionary ranks of flamethrowers with words. Baldwin was now linked to Ralph Ellison and rebuked by Baraka for his objection to protest literature. "Baldwin . . . later refutes his own arguments by becoming a civil rights spokesman and activist in the sixties and with *Blues for Mr. Charlie* he has even begun to question the nonviolent, passive pseudo-revolution put forward by the black bourgeoisie through its most articulate spokesman, Dr. Martin Luther King, Jr.," Baraka wrote.

Three years later, at Baldwin's funeral, Baraka was at his rhetorical best, joining a host of notables in eulogizing Baldwin. From the speeches came loads of information about Baldwin that wasn't widely known. Some complained that a Tuesday afternoon memorial service was inconvenient for the common, workaday folks who loved Baldwin. Still, it did not stop the massive number who forsook job and other appointments to say goodbye to their native son, a son who had in so many ways celebrated their lives, and who now gathered to celebrate his. In his reflection, the writer and Professor Clyde Taylor captured the rhythm of the moment, recalling the drums of passion from "Babatunde Olatunji and his ensemble in white akbadas in short sleeves . . . their sound resonated through the awesome structure." The celestial voice of Odetta swept across the congregation, and her version of "Sometimes I Feel Like a Motherless Child" and her mournful elegy would set the stage for the reflections that flowed from the treasury of words emitted by Maya Angelou, Toni Morrison, and Amiri Baraka.

I turned to the notes I scribbled and later published in the

Michigan Chronicle about the service: Authors Angelou and Morrison also offered rhapsodic encomiums. "You have been like a brother to me," Angelou said of Baldwin, "[you] know black women need brothers." In the flowery prose that signifies her novels, Morrison recalled that "no one powered or inhabited the language the way you did for me. In your hands, language was handsome again. We saw it as it was meant to be . . . you brought us to ourselves." She added that she needed Baldwin "to tell me what I am feeling."

France's ambassador to the United States, Emmanuel de Margerie, compared Baldwin to the great French writers. "He was regarded in the land of Voltaire and Zola as a man of principle and dedication. He was a spokesman for his people."

During his turn at the podium—nearly forty minutes of exquisite oratory—Baraka recalled when he had first met Baldwin at Howard University in 1955 at the debut performance of *The Amen Corner*, directed by Owen Dodson. "But it was not until later confined in the armed forces that I got to feel that spirit from another more desperate angle of need, and therefore understanding," he recited. A few in the audience expressed some doubt about his sincerity, knowing of his past repudiation of Baldwin. Whether disingenuous or not, it was hard not be moved by a poet operating at the top of his game. When he announced that "Jimmy was God's black revolutionary mouth" there was an explosion of applause in the sanctuary, and Baraka, to a great degree it seemed, had redeemed himself even with those who found it difficult to accept that he and Baldwin had become increasingly fond of each other with each passing year.

Baraka almost in tears roared: "He was my older brother—a brother of communal spirit!"

Baldwin's mother cried out: "Jimmy, Jimmy, no, no. We need you now."

Toward the end of the service, which must have taken more than three hours, there was a moment of eerie silence before Baldwin's voice was heard in a recording. "Precious Lord, take my hand, lead me on, let me stand . . ." Baldwin sang a cappella for the most part, and the intonation, the mellow baritone was unmistakable. "It was Jimmy making his own final comment, as always finding the best word for the occasion," Taylor concluded. The Prodigal Son had returned home to sing his song in his native land.

Escorted by the police, the forty-car funeral cortege weaved its way slowly through Harlem, passing a few blocks from where Baldwin once lived and went to school. Then the freeway to Ferncliff Cemetery for burial.

A few of Baldwin's close associates, rather than venture to the cemetery, chose instead to retire to Mikell's, one of Baldwin's favorite haunts, to remember him in song and drink.

Afterword

A recent, casual survey of Harlem found very few signs of Baldwin's legacy. Unlike Duke Ellington, Mary McLeod Bethune, John Russwurm, Claude Brown, Adam Clayton Powell, Jr., Frederick Douglass, John Henrik Clarke, Tito Puente, Harriet Tubman, and Baldwin's rival and friend Malcolm X (El Hajj Malik El Shabazz), there is no statue, no school, park, place, square, or street named after James Baldwin, and only one plaque that has been affixed inside P.S. 24, the first school he attended. To have an intersection in his honor would seem to be a minor task. Even the composer Scott Joplin, whose residency in Harlem was extremely brief, has a marker outside the last placed he lived.

Baldwin's name is enshrined on the Walk of Fame on 135th Street—but embedded in the sidewalk. His memory is trampled upon daily and barely noticed by pedestrians more prone to spill coffee there than to stop and pay homage.

However, Baldwin is getting some recognition beyond Harlem, just as fellow luminary Paul Robeson had a mountain named after him in Russia, and a shrine pays tribute to musician John Coltrane in Japan. I was a reporter on the occasion in Harlem at the Schomburg Center in July 2004 when the U.S. Postal Service unveiled a commemorative stamp honoring Baldwin. Now, like those of Paul Robeson, Langston Hughes, and Malcolm X, Baldwin's visage adorns a stamp, and in the background there is a street scene straight out of Harlem. It was a moving tribute. Baldwin's family, particularly his sister Gloria and his brother George, beamed with pride and their eyes seemed to glisten with each accolade from Ruby Dee, Ossie Davis, Amiri Baraka, and Maya Angelou. Recalling her first days with Baldwin, Angelou said, "He was my rainbow in the clouds. He still is, and will ever be!"

Reading from Baldwin's "Stranger in the Village," in *Notes of a Native Son*, the late Ossie Davis related some of the writer's poignant insight on America's race relations: "People who shut their eyes to reality simply invite their own destruction, and anyone who insists on remaining in a state of innocence long after that innocence is dead turns himself into a monster." Perhaps for effect, Davis made a very deliberate pause then concluded, with rolling thunder, "Thus spoke the prophet."

On March 29, 2006, Princeton University's Kwame Anthony Appiah, the Laurance S. Rockefeller University Professor of Philosophy and the University Center for Human Values, delivered the inaugural address in the Program in African American Studies' James Baldwin Lecture Series. When Dr. Michael Eric Dyson wrote an article for *Ebony* magazine (November 2005) on "What America Would Be Like" without sixty years of black contributions, James Baldwin was the first person he mentioned. Countless articles, essays, and speeches have referenced Baldwin; he comes up in crossword puzzles and quizzes. In 1985 a film version of *Go Tell It on the Mountain* was made starring Paul Winfield, James Bond III, Rosalind Cash, and Olivia Cole. It was aired on PBS.

And we should cite the creativity of writer and choreographer Ralph Lemon and the splendid use of Baldwin in his recent installation at the Kitchen Gallery in New York City. Among the more notable discussions of Baldwin is Henry Louis Gates, Jr.'s introductory essay in *The Annotated Uncle Tom's Cabin* (2006), which Gates edited with Hollis Robbins. To a great extent, Baldwin is the whipping boy as Gates revisits the controversial essay "Everybody's Protest Novel," in which a rather overwrought Baldwin eviscerates Harriet Beecher Stowe's nineteenth-century classic. Though Gates offers some snide remarks about Baldwin's homosexuality, there are few revelations here. And few critics have done as much as Baldwin did himself to reframe his critique of 1949.

At the crux of Gates's reassessment is Baldwin's denouncement of *Uncle Tom's Cabin* on the basis of its sentimentality and Baldwin's linking of that trait to the melodrama of Richard Wright's *Native Son*. Just as Baldwin uses Stowe to get at Wright, Gates uses Baldwin's attack to form the bulwark of his defense of Stowe, as we will see below.

It must have been Stowe's sentimentality that first attracted Baldwin to the novel, which he read many times as a youngster, only to lambaste it much later. Stowe's book, in my estimation, may have been an easy and convenient target for Baldwin in his inexorable march toward recognition. In an interview with Jordan Elgrably and George Plimpton in 1984, Baldwin said that when he wrote the critique he thought he was dealing with Wright, but he was really thinking about Stowe. "Richard's *Native Son* was the only contemporary representation there was of a black person in America," he said, which in itself is quite an incredible conclusion. "One of the reasons I wrote what I did about [*Native Son*] is a technical objection, which I uphold today."

Wright certainly felt he was the target, not Stowe, and received the essay as a betrayal of their friendship. Baldwin may have not intended to condemn Wright—and he would make such an assertion years later—but his subsequent actions, especially his essay "Many Thousands Gone," indicate he was still out to extinguish his mentor. But Gates is more concerned and indeed is rather preoccupied with Baldwin's disparaging of Stowe. (Gates might have had the chance to ask Baldwin about some of these issues in 1973, when he was fortunate enough to catch up with Baldwin at his home in southern France. However, the full account of that meeting, which also included Josephine Baker, remains unpublished.)

The points of contention raised by Gates are by no means new. Almost every critic worth his or her salt has grappled with Baldwin's essay, though Gates does not cite any of them. Gates is less interested in Baldwin's dismissal of Wright, and this may be appropriate since Wright and *Native Son* are mentioned only once and then toward the end of the essay. A paramount concern for him in this introduction, portions of which appeared in the *New York Times Book Review*, is the matter of sex. When Baldwin writes that Tom has been "robbed of his humanity and divested of his sex," Gates finds his productive tangent. To make his point, Gates takes Baldwin's comment about sex out of context: Baldwin's metaphor may have had more of a religious intention than anything else. It is not enough, it seems, that Baldwin was

equating blackness with sin and whiteness with grace, innocence, purity for Gates to drive home his sexual theme of
Uncle Tom and blonde Little Eva. But even Gates apparently
realized how much of a speculative leap it is to connote anything sexual between the black man and the white girl–there
is, however, Gates concedes, a physical relationship between
them.

Gates returns to Baldwin's main objection to Stowe's
novel: her sentimentality. When Gates suggests that in his
novels and plays Baldwin was guilty of the very thing he
accused Stowe of, Gates joins a multitude of critics who have
arrived at the same conclusion. "When Baldwin looked in
the mirror of his literary antecedents," Gates wrote in his
final paragraph of the *Times* excerpt, "what he saw, to his
horror, was Harriet Beecher Stowe in blackface. Stowe's
most vigorous detractor was destined to become her true
20th century literary heir." In the quest to stake his literary
turf, Baldwin may have anticipated the wrath from critics of
his novels, plays, and short stories, but it is doubtful he would
have ever perceived himself as Harriet Beecher Stowe in
blackface.

Baldwin, it can be said at last, is a convenience for Gates,
who might have found an even more useful critic in Martin
Delany, but Delany is virtually unknown. We see a utility to
Baldwin's legacy, no matter how old and shopworn an essay
he wrote when he was in his twenties.

Still, Gates and others have every right to evoke Baldwin's
majesty for their own purposes. That is just another indication of his staying power these many years after his death, of
the enduring power of Baldwin's words. Of his books, *Go
Tell It on the Mountain* is by far the most popular. It was

recently selected by the Chicago libraries as a book of choice, especially for young black men struggling with parental authority and their own sense of selfhood.

And the power of James Baldwin's words will have to do until everybody knows his name, particularly on the streets of Harlem, where he gathered the realities of his odyssey through occupied territory.

Acknowledgments

I was not thinking about James Baldwin one afternoon when James Fitzgerald called and proposed doing a biography on Baldwin. My first reaction was to ask if we really need another look at his life, since there are already several very fine biographies, though none are of recent vintage. I concluded there was little I could add to works on Baldwin by W. J. Weatherby, David Leeming, Ted Gottfried, and James Campbell. But Fitzgerald persisted. We tossed about a number of possible approaches, angles that would be different from the other published works. It dawned on me that one of things that hadn't been fully discussed in any of the bios was Baldwin's relationship to Harlem. While each biography could not ignore Baldwin's history in Harlem, there was still no exhaustive account of his early years in Harlem or how that community figured in his fiction and nonfiction. Nor were his often cantankerous encounters with several Harlem figures thoroughly examined. Fleshing these out would not only place them in larger relief but at the same time provide more angles on Baldwin's complexity.

We agreed, in consultation with my agent of record, Marie Brown, that such a probe might be rewarding. After completing the proposal on what we called *Baldwin's Harlem*, there was the matter of convincing an editor to take on the project. Once the proposal was in Malaika Adero's hands, she didn't blink. Malaika threw her considerable support behind the book, as well as her critical judgment. So, my agents, Brown and Fitzgerald, and my editor, Malaika, were there at the beginning and at the end of this quest. Their advice continues to resonate.

To list all those who came to my aid would cover far too many pages, but there is no way I could have begun this journey without the endorsement of Gloria and George, two of Baldwin's siblings. Right from the first words, G and G gave me a thumbs-up, letting me know they had my back. Because she has her own Baldwin project under way, Gloria could not give me the kind of time I desired, but she made sure that George was there to fill me in on the family's early years.

Living in Harlem places me in immediate contact with so many Harlemites who knew Baldwin and have eagerly conveyed some of their impressions and memories. Quincy and Margaret Troupe, the esteemed Percy Sutton, Sharon Howard at the Schomburg Center, the late Dr. John Henrik Clarke, Stretch Johnson, Mel Tapley, Preston Wilcox, the estimable Elombe Brath, Gil Noble, Greg Tate, Jules Allen, Woodie King, Jr., Shirley Scott, Florence Rice, Sonia Sanchez, Playthell Benjamin, Sondra Kathryn Wilson, Bill and Susan Tatum, Cat Boyd, Peniel Joseph, Cleophus Roseboro, Michael Dinwiddie, Amiri Baraka, Jerry Gafio Watts, James DeJongh, Mike Thelwell, Gloria Thomas, Malik Chaka, and Fred Beauford all provided moments of inspiration and/or information that pushed this endeavor to completion. A special shout-out is extended to Tom Pitoniak for his sharp eye and superb editorial support. Of course, they are not responsible for anything beyond attribution. The two people I talked to most are Robert Van Lierop, my lifelong comrade as well as my attorney, and my wife, Elza; both provided me with indispensable food for thought and otherwise. Between the two of them I am assured of more than a modicum of protection legally and grammatically. Both are near and dear to me, and without their constancy this book would still be languishing somewhere in the ether, waiting for that final word.

I wish I knew all the names of all the librarians, booksellers (and vendors), clerks, and researchers who seemed to be ever at my beck and call. Only here are you nameless, and all of you are certainly blameless, though, in so many important ways, you were indispensable.

Finally, there is my gratitude to the Baldwin scholars who turned the sod to make this crop grow and hopefully prosper. Your spade work made it possible for me to work a furrow without too much effort and frustration. I was just the man with the hoe, nurturing another sprig of Baldwin to life and possibility.

To James: It is hoped that in some small way another aspect of your glorious stay with us is revealed in these pages. This was by no means an attempt to capture the rapture of your days in a neat biography or to distill all that has been said about you—for the most part, you have spoken most eloquently for yourself. And in a larger, much more definitive way you spoke for all of us, on a number of critical measures and frequencies.

INTERVIEWS

Interview with Michael Thelwell

October 31, 2006

As an emerging writer some years ago, Michael Thelwell, currently the chair of the Afro-American Studies Department at the University of Massachusetts at Amherst and an acclaimed author, admitted his admiration for James Baldwin. But unlike so many of us who longed for an opportunity to catch just a glimpse of Baldwin, let alone to command some of his valuable time in conversation, Thelwell spent many hours in his company. Many of their late-night and early-morning exchanges occurred while Baldwin was teaching at the area's Five Colleges (comprising Amherst, Hampshire, Mount Holyoke, Smith, and UMass), mainly at UMass. It was at Thelwell's initiative that Baldwin agreed to come to the university to receive an honorary degree in the late seventies. The occasion for Baldwin was so rewarding that he agreed again to a brief teaching residency. In this telephone interview, Thelwell recounts some of those meetings as well as his studied opinion of Baldwin's legacy and his reaction to a few of his detractors. It should be noted that we had no idea during our discussion of William Styron that he was only a few hours from his death on November 1. He was eighty-one.

Herb: Let me begin by saying how much I have enjoyed your work over the years, and your particularly ardent defense of Baldwin. I have just finished reading your review of James Campbell's biography of Baldwin, *Talking at the Gates* [1991], a review that appeared in *Transition* in 1992, entitled "A Prophet Is Not Without Honor." In the review you do a little more than taking Campbell to task; it's a quantum-sized drubbing, yet on the back of the book there is your blurb commending it. What's up with that?

Michael: I was not aware of that. I certainly don't recall writing one, which means they may have taken it out of the *Transition* article . . . or the *Boston Globe* review. What does it say?

Herb: It reads: "A life-sized portrait in very bold strokes . . . A lively book that is immensely readable, serious, careful, and informed." This was apparently published from a review you did for the *Boston Sunday Globe*.

Michael: Oh, Jesus. Part of that language might have been added by the editors.

Herb: Mike, given your close association with Baldwin, why haven't you written a biography of him?

Michael: There is a very good biography already by David Leeming. I reviewed it for the *Boston Globe*. At one time I was considering writing a memoir, a biography but the one editor I talked to about it was not very interested, so I let it drop. I may get around to it someday.

Herb: Did Baldwin talk much about Harlem during those evenings you spent with him?

Michael: He didn't talk about Harlem per se, that is, Harlem as a community. But he did talk about his childhood, boyhood experiences. Let me back up on this and set the stage for you. This has to be handled with precision. I was having a conversation just the other day with a friend who was visiting me and we discussed how [Ralph] Ellison and Albert Murray took issue with Baldwin because of the way he described Harlem. I think I understand what their concern was: they were boosters for black culture and black accomplishment–Harlem and its unique presence in the American landscape. They expressed an interest in the music of Duke Ellington and jazz in general and Baldwin never spoke about Harlem in these terms. He referred to the music and jazz obliquely but he never put it in the context of being at the center of black culture and civilization. What many people fail to understand is that Jimmy was *in* but not *of* Harlem. You see, both Ellison and Murray did not grow up in Harlem like Jimmy.

Herb: That's a good point because Ellison came to Harlem from Alabama via Oklahoma and Murray from Tennessee via Alabama. And they were lifelong friends. Murray still lives in Harlem and turned ninety back in the spring. Ellison died in 1994 but wrote most of *Invisible Man* while living in Harlem. So your point is well taken.

Michael: Unlike Jimmy, they came to New York as adults. They were attracted here, I believe, because of Harlem's mythology, the veneer of the [Harlem] renaissance. For Jimmy, Harlem was a place where he lived. When I say he was *in* Harlem but not *of* it, you have to look at his first novel, *Go Tell It on the Mountain*. First of all, most of it takes place within the circles of the sanctified church whose members are from the old country, the American South. What I'm saying is that the universe is bounded by the terms, values, and perceptions of the sanctified church. The members are very sanctimonious, narrow-minded, and exclusionary, and very rigid in their morality. To the extent there is a white presence, it is an ominous brooding white presence; it is never explicitly evoked in the novel. It's like the novels of Zora Neale Hurston—you don't see any white people but you feel their presence. When you look at the geography of that novel, it is narrowly divided between the community of the saints and the sinners. Everything outside of the church is the world, the flesh, and the devil. Then there's the sexuality and homosexuality on the threshing floor . . .

Herb: Yes, that's the book's third part. It begins with "The Seventh Day," and then there's "The Prayers of the Saints."

Michael: In any event, what I'm suggesting to you is that Jimmy grew up in this very closed community. In this context, you are either a saint or you are out there in the world. So you see, the Harlem that Ellison and Murray celebrate would be of the streets—sinful, wicked, and debased. It's a world that they avoided. Jimmy was in Harlem, which is the world, the flesh, and the devil, but, in reality, he was in a community of saints. For him the streets represented the cops, the hustlers, the whores, and a host of other sexual temptations that were to be reviled and avoided. Then he went to this junior high school, Frederick Douglass, and here he was taken out of Harlem downtown to the library by that white woman . . .

Herb: Orilla Miller.

Michael: Yes. And there was Countee Cullen who taught English there. When he starts to get out in the world, he goes downtown to the library with a white woman who's taking him to the museum and to plays. But he's not taken to Harlem for this kind of cultural exposure.

Herb: They did take him to the Lafayette Theatre. That's where he saw "Voodoo *Macbeth*" directed by Orson Welles and starring Canada Lee. So there was at least some exposure to culture in Harlem. But that's about the extent of it, which doesn't disturb your point at all.

Michael: Exactly. It makes it more accurate. Then he goes to DeWitt Clinton High School in the Bronx, which is a lot like Bronx Science where the best students attend.

Herb: Where Kwame Ture [Stokely Carmichael] went, whom you knew so well, having worked with him on the completion of his autobiography after his death.

Michael: And Kwame received a similar kind of experience where you're surrounded with progressive, artistic kids. At DeWitt Clinton, there was Richard Avedon, the famous photographer; Sol Stein and Emile Capouya and others. Most of them were Jewish. Then there was his [Baldwin's] association with the artist Beauford Delaney, who became his mentor and introduced him to that world. So, he went from Harlem to a high school with those white, bright Jewish kids, then on to Beauford Delaney and Greenwich Village and the bohemian scene. By this route, he kind of bypassed Harlem, but still he was now in the world of temptation and debasement. Then there was the intellectual world that included such leftist journals as *Partisan Review, Commentary* and the *New Leader.* There he developed his politics, his social criticism. He was moving in vaguely leftist, vaguely progressive, vaguely avant-garde artistic circles of New York, which had very little to do with Harlem.

Herb: But something must be said about the presence of Harlem in his nonfiction, if it was hardly present in his fiction, don't you think?

Michael: I'm not saying Harlem is not there, but it's the way that it's there that Murray objects to. Baldwin did not extol the cultural wealth and influence of Harlem on the rest of the world.

Herb: But there are instances in which Baldwin does extol the cultural wealth of Harlem.

Michael: Well, to that degree, then, Murray's argument is wrong.

Herb: And that's one of the points I make in the book as I challenge some of Murray's assumptions he put forth in his book *The Omni-Americans.* I was curious to know if Baldwin ever said anything about Ellison or Murray to you.

Michael: We discussed Ellison a couple of times. There is one story he told me. At one point, very early in his career—and it really speaks to Ellison's absurd notion of what a literary artist was. Jimmy had come back from France, having completed *Go Tell It on the Mountain,* and was working on that marvelous novel, *Giovanni's Room,* the most beautifully written and constructed of all his novels . . . and it took great courage to publish such a novel at that time.

Herb: He was told that to publish this book with such a prominence of homosexuality would destroy his career . . .

Michael: Precisely. Well, anyway, to get back to Ellison, Jimmy had come back to America because of the civil rights movement and what was happening to black people. Jimmy had gone to meet Dr. King and wrote that fabulous essay on him.

Herb: That was the essay entitled "The Dangerous Road Before Martin Luther King, Jr." I think it was written in 1961 when he traveled to Atlanta.

Michael: Ellison drove him back to the airport after that meeting. And he said that all the way to the airport Ellison was hectoring him. "Baldwin," Ellison told him, "this is a great mistake you're making, getting involved in the civil rights movement. The artist must maintain a certain esthetic distance; the artist, at times, must be aloof from the struggle. This is a bad mistake you're making and it's likely to destroy your objectivity as an artist and ruin your career." Baldwin said he kept lecturing him and lecturing him. So, I asked Jimmy, what did he do? He said, "I went." And look at Ellison. He ended up with one novel and a collection of essays. Meanwhile, Baldwin went on to become a witness, an eloquent voice for the aspirations of black Americans. I told him that if he had followed Ellison's advice and kept an artistic distance he might have been equally bankrupt and barren as a writer. We both laughed.

Herb: There's another writer that I'm curious to know how

Baldwin felt [about], and that's William Styron. Since you were very close to Baldwin and Baldwin was close to Styron, and you were among a coterie of writers who were outraged by Styron's book *The Confessions of Nat Turner*, I was wondering if that put you in an awkward position?

Michael: Not really. There was no problem. You certainly can see Jimmy's influence on Styron since he spent time with him while he was writing that book. Later, however, I did ask him if it had changed his position. He would never admit that he had changed his position. What he did say was that at that time he had been living with Styron, and was leaving the country, and Baldwin asked him would he take over the Tony Maynard case . . .

Herb: This was one of Baldwin's young friends who had been accused of murder and to whom Baldwin felt a deep obligation to support.

Michael: Precisely. And so while he never changed his mind about the book he did tell me that because of the things mentioned about [it] he felt obligated to defend Styron.

Herb: I think Baldwin addressed this matter in the introduction he wrote to your book, right?

Michael: I don't rightly recall . . .

Herb: In effect, he said that if other writers have a problem with Styron's interpretation then they ought to write their own. He said that it wasn't his position to tell another writer what to write, that far too often people had been trying to tell him what to write. I think he even accepted your point about Styron's distortions of Turner's life, and that for him to do so was one of the prerogatives and necessities of fiction.

Michael: I don't think Jimmy would agree with that characterization.

Herb: Mike, as we move to the conclusion of this interview, I want to read a passage to you from one of your essays: "And slender, gay James Baldwin taught a generation of us how to be black men in this country, and he gave us a language in which to engage the struggle. Which is why if the generation of black writers see and reach any further, it is because we stand on those narrow but durable shoulders." To me, of all the paradoxes of his life, this may be the most significant one.

Michael: It may not be the most significant one, but I certainly set it up with the intent to show that paradox.

Herb: Writing paradoxically was certainly an obvious trait to his style, but what about contradictions, Mike?

Michael: I have a long take on that in the review I addressed to Mr. Campbell. Your readers can check that out.

Herb: And finally, what about Baldwin's legacy? You look around Harlem, and other than a sidewalk marker on 135th Street, there is not any indication that Baldwin lived here. There are no streets, parks, or monuments to his memory. Even the school he attended, the students who go there or who have gone there have no idea that such a famous writer once walked through those doors, sat in those classrooms.

Michael: This is certainly something that must be raised, and it must be raised very powerfully.

Interview with Quincy Troupe

Poet and author Quincy Troupe has lived off and on for more than three decades in various neighborhoods in New York City, including Harlem. In 1987, two weeks before Baldwin's death, he traveled to the south of France to visit the writer and to conduct his last interview with him. Nearly twenty years after Baldwin's death, Troupe reflects on the writer and his impact on American letters.

Herb: This book has mainly been centered on Baldwin's relationship, his connection to Harlem and a few significant individuals from that community, but something more, I feel, should be said about Baldwin the writer. How do you view him as a writer?

Quincy: For me, James Baldwin wrote the truest American sentence in the twentieth century. He had a sentence that reflected his voice. When you heard him speak, when you read his work . . . he had it fashioned in such a way that his sentence was his voice. I think some of his essays are the best ever written in this country. I think *Go Tell It on the Mountain* is a masterpiece. I divide it into two parts; "The Seventh Day" is marvelous, but the second part doesn't quite measure up, but it's all right.

Herb: To what extent do you believe that Baldwin, having been born in Harlem, was circumscribed by this background, this beginning? I guess what I'm trying to determine is the impact of geography on his writing. Ralph Ellison often said that geography was fate.

Quincy: I certainly believe this is true. Look, I'm from St. Louis and you're originally from Detroit, so we have a Midwest experience that would be different from Baldwin's since he was here in New York City and running into all kinds of people. His environment was much more international than ours, so he had to be ready for different kinds of people and their cultures. For me, coming up in St. Louis, it was black and white. But Baldwin was confronted with a multitude of realities that came from a diverse mixture of ethnic groups. This gave him a larger, global perspective on people and their culture.

Herb: Currently, here in Harlem, the wave of gentrification has practically inundated the community. What do you think Baldwin's impressions would be about these developments?

Quincy: If African Americans controlled these new developments, I think Jimmy would feel a lot better about it. When a place begins to fall apart it has to be gentrified. Disrepair is rampant in Harlem and there's nothing hip about that. I remember when I first moved in here, on 116th Street there was nothing but garbage cans and junkies standing over them. Right over there, that little triangle of land was called "Needle Park" because there were some junkies hanging around there and just about everywhere. I think Baldwin would want to see things improved, but under our control. We should have controlled it, but we didn't.

I'm an artist and writer, not a real estate developer, so that's not my job. That's the responsibility of black politicians, bankers, and businessmen and -women.

Herb: What about the clubs? There was the recent reopening of Minton's Playhouse where bebop was born and nurtured . . .

Quincy: Jimmy would want that under black control, too. In that way, it would be under our control and we could bring in top-caliber musicians and pay them a righteous amount of money. We need a first-class establishment that will compare with the clubs downtown.

Herb: But it is black-owned . . .

Quincy: But it still hasn't brought in the top-drawer performers, the best of the jazz musicians. It's got to be first class; you can't be half-stepping on this. Jimmy would want the place to have that same aura, the same class it had when he used to stop by. I think he would have agreed with some of the changes, but it all goes back to vision.

Herb: How would he have felt about the current literary scene in Harlem?

Quincy: He would have probably wanted it to be much stronger than it is. I think he would have wanted more attention paid to our elders, and I don't mean to dis the young, but something has to be done to tie the generations together. The Schomburg and the Countee Cullen Library—and you know Baldwin haunted Harlem's libraries—are doing some positive things in this direction, but we need to do this across the community. All the other groups—Asians, Jews, Hispanics, even our newly arrived Africans—have created ways to incorporate their elders into the ongoing affairs, but we haven't. It's one of our flaws.

Herb: Where can some of the blame be placed for this flaw?

Quincy: The library system in Harlem can take some of the blame; it can be faulted. The people who run the system haven't been creative or visionary enough to find the money they need, and I know they are always complaining about the lack of funds. But there are plenty of well-to-do people here in Harlem that I'm sure would be willing to donate, if they were pursued. Both of us should be invited from time to time to speak at the various branches, our books should be available and on display. This is one of the things the community has to do and we have to find ways to apply the pressure to make this happen.

Herb: Quincy, you have the unique experience of being close to two African American giants: James Baldwin and Miles Davis. Is there a common thread . . .

Quincy: Somebody brought James to a party at Miles's house and this is when they first met. Initially they liked each other, but Miles was always suspicious of writers. It was a color thing. You see, both of them were dark. And once Miles told me that he liked James because he was little and dark, "just like me," he said. Both of them felt they had been looked down on by light-skinned blacks. Plus, they were both geniuses, outspoken, and they were radical. Some have even suggested that there was a homosexual hookup between them. This is what I heard, although no one ever talked to me about that.

Herb: Now James visited Miles. Did Miles visit Baldwin?

Quincy: Miles liked Baldwin so much that whenever he went to France he would block out a week in his schedule when he wasn't playing and just wanted to relax, to go down to Baldwin's house in southern France. There was a great restaurant up the street from Baldwin's house called the Colombe d'Or, one of the finest restaurants in the world. They would often go there to eat and to drink. Sometimes they were the only patrons in the place; there were times when they wanted to be alone. I think they genuinely loved each other, loved each other's work, and loved each other's company. Sometimes Miles would bring his girlfriend and they would really enjoy each other.

Herb: In terms of Baldwin's legacy, what shape is it in today? And you've edited a book that addresses this matter extensively. You look around the community and there are statues, plaques, streets, parks, and schools named after people, but other than a sidewalk marker on 135th Street there's no indication that Baldwin ever lived here. Is there anything we can do about this oversight?

Quincy: Yes, and this is the kind of thing we have to do, we writers, musicians, artists . . . something we have to do. We have to advocate and push for that, and not only here in New York but everywhere. Look, they have a street named after Pedro Pietri, the Puerto Rican poet down on the Lower East Side, but there's nothing here for Baldwin. We need to be able to stand in front of our young people and point to a statue and tell them who it is and what they were about. We should be able to tell them "This is James Baldwin Street . . ." and give them a short history of what he did and who he was. This is something we have to do and it's about time we did it.

CHRONOLOGY OF MAJOR EVENTS IN JAMES BALDWIN'S LIFE

Born in Harlem Hospital, New York City, August 2, son of Emma Berdis Jones	1924
Emma Berdis Jones marries David Baldwin	1927
George Baldwin born in January	1928
Barbara Baldwin, named after her paternal grandmother, born in August	1929
Wilmer (Lover) Baldwin born in October	1930
David Baldwin, Jr. born in December	1931
Gloria Baldwin born	1933
Graduates from Public School 24 in Harlem	1935
Ruth Baldwin born	
Edits and contributes to school magazine, the *Douglass Pilot*	1937–38
Elizabeth Baldwin born	1937
Graduates from Frederick Douglass Junior High School in Harlem	1938
Undergoes religious experience at Mount Calvary of the Pentecostal Faith Church	

Preaches at the Fireside Pentecostal Assembly	1938–41
Attends DeWitt Clinton High School in the Bronx, graduating January 29, 1942	1938–42
Begins first draft of *Go Tell It on the Mountain*	1942
Edits and contributes to the *Magpie,* school magazine at DeWitt Clinton	1940–41
Works in New Jersey and encounters overt white racism	1942–43
David Baldwin, Sr. dies July 29	1943
Paula Maria born July 29	
Lives and works in Greenwich Village	1943–48
Meets Richard Wright, who secures for him a Eugene F. Saxton Memorial Trust Award	1944–45
Begins publishing reviews in the *Nation* and the *New Leader*	1947
Rosenwald Fellowship	1948
Sails for Europe on a one-way ticket, November 11	
Lives in Paris, Switzerland, and the south of France	1948–57
Meets Lucien Happersberger	1949–50
Go Tell It on the Mountain	1953
Guggenheim Fellowship	1954
Awarded fellowship to attend MacDowell Colony	
Notes of a Native Son	1955
He attends opening night of *The Amen Corner* at Howard University	1956
Receives a grant from the National Institute of Arts and Letters and a Fellowship from Partisan Review	
Giovanni's Room	
Returns in July to United States to live	1957

In fall visits the South for the first time

Works at the Actors Studio with director Elia Kazan	1958–59
Ford Foundation grant-in-aid	1959
Nobody Knows My Name	1961

Drama critic for the *Urbanite*

Another Country	1962
The Fire Next Time	1963

Lectures widely on civil rights

Meets with U.S. Attorney General Robert Kennedy, May 24

Participates in March on Washington, August 28

Blues for Mr. Charlie opens at the ANTA Theatre on Broadway, April 23	1964

Nothing Personal (with Richard Avedon)

Going to Meet the Man	1965
Lives in Europe and Turkey	1965–67
Tell Me How Long the Train's Been Gone	1968
A Rap on Race (with Margaret Mead)	1971
No Name in the Street	1972

One Day, When I Was Lost

A Dialogue (with Nikki Giovanni)	1973
If Beale Street Could Talk	1974
The Devil Finds Work	1976

Little Man, Little Man: A Story of Childhood

Just Above My Head	1979
Jimmy's Blues: Selected Poems	1983
Introduction to the new edition of *Notes of a Native Son*	1984
The Evidence of Things Not Seen	1985

The Price of the Ticket   1985

Receives the French Legion of Honor from President
    François Mitterrand in June   1986

Baldwin dies of pancreatic cancer in St. Paul de Vence,
    France, December 1   1987

Buried at Ferncliff Cemetery in Hartsdale, New York

Berdis Baldwin dies at ninety-nine years of age and is
    buried in the same cemetery as her son   1999

Notes

Chapter 1: Born in Harlem

2 "absorbed the full impact": Telephone interview with Gloria Karefa-Smart, April 10, 2006.

3 a massive parade: Tony Martin, *Literary Garveyism: Garvey, Black Arts and the Harlem Renaissance* (Dover, Mass.: Majority Press), pp. 75–76. Martin is not exactly sure about the date though he speculates that the parade must have occurred after August 1. (Actually, the parade with some 3,500 marchers did occur on Friday, August 1, according to a story in the *New York Times*, and Garvey, out on bail, was guarded by men with "shining sabres." Moreover, the August 9th edition of the *Negro World*, a paper published by the Universal Negro Improvement Association, covered the convention exhaustively. The quote is taken from a rather "flippant" account by Hurston, which she titled "The Emperor Effaces Himself," and was nothing more than another bit of satire to further her "entry into the mainstream of white acceptance," Martin notes. One wonders how Garvey would have fared in the play she had planned with Paul Green, in which Garvey along with Father Divine and other larger-than-life figures, would be fused with the folk legend John De Conqueror.

3   "A black boy born": James Baldwin, "Dark Days," in *The Price of the Ticket* (New York: St. Martin's Press, 1985), p. 659.

4   "It did not take me long": Baldwin, "No Name in the Street," in *The Price of the Ticket,* p. 451.

4   "George in January": Ibid., p. 452.

5   "You see?": James Baldwin, *"The Devil Finds Work,"* p. 560. Of all his books, Baldwin seemed to be less optimistic about the success of *The Devil Finds Work*. In a letter to his brother, David, on March 8, 1975, he expressed this lack of confidence. "Why is it that you always discover, too late, when the book is almost over—and cannot be written again—that you are, absolutely, the world's worst writer, have no talent at all? I cannot imagine anybody reading this book, either it, or I must leave this house. That means I'm scared shitless, am about to turn it in. It's either very good or very bad, it's not like anything I've ever done before, and I just don't know." From Schomburg Center, Baldwin file.

5   "embody the power": Robert Farris Thompson, *Flash of the Spirit* (New York: Vintage, 1983), p. 28. Thinking of Baldwin's face, I am reminded of writer Julian Mayfield's article "And Then Came Baldwin," published in *Harlem, U.S.A.,* John Henrik Clarke, ed. (New York: Collier, 1971). "One can't help thinking about Baldwin's face," Mayfield wrote. "I have never seen any face like it which was not the product of one of our American slums. Looking at it I could understand why the word 'terror' so often crops up in his descriptions of his childhood. His face has nothing to do with genetics; it could only have been chiseled by the city, in the muck and shadows of tenements, where children learn early that disaster can strike at any time from any quarter, from the cop on the beat, the gang around the corner, or from one's own bitter and disillusioned parents. Baldwin's is the face of the little street scrapper, sweeping the horizon with his radar antenna (those eyes) ever alert for a sign of danger" (p. 165).

5 "By 1920": Gilbert Osofsky, *Harlem: The Making of a Ghetto: Negro New York, 1890–1930* (New York: Harper & Row, 1971), p. 123.

6 "Harlem was not": Baldwin, "Dark Days," p. 660. Father Divine's International Peace Mission Movement was an infamous cult but a life-saving institution for many starving Harlemites. Perhaps the most memorable incident related to Divine and his movement occurred in 1931 and it furthered his already growing notoriety. On November 13, when a gaggle of supporters and their cars assembled around his home in Sayville, a hamlet in Long Island, he was arrested for disturbing the peace. He pled not guilty, refused bail, and was subsequently tried and convicted; however, the jury asked for leniency. This request was ignored and Divine was sentenced to one year in jail and fined five hundred dollars. Two days later the judge, who showed no signs of sickness, dropped dead. Seizing the opportunity, Divine said the judge's death was not the result of natural causes. According to reports, a Divine follower had announced to others at the trial that the judge had signed his own death warrant. "He can't live long now," the follower reportedly said. "He's offended Almighty God." Not missing a beat, Divine said from his cell: "I hated to do it!"

7 "There were British West Indians": Rudolph Fisher, "Ringtail," in Herb Boyd, ed., *The Harlem Reader* (New York: Three Rivers Press, 2003), p. 55.

11 "Five thousand Harlemites": Mark Naison, *Communists in Harlem During the Depression* (New York: Grove Press, 1984), p. 60.

12 "A large mass of Negroes": Anna Arnold Hedgeman, *The Trumpet Sounds: A Memoir of Negro Leadership* (New York: Holt, Rinehart & Winston, 1964), pp. 56–57. Barbara Ransby, in her remarkable biography *Ella Baker and The Black Freedom Movement: A Radical Democratic Vision* (Chapel Hill:

University of North Carolina Press, 2003), has an informative chapter on Harlem in the 1930s that examines Ella Baker's activism.

12 "some of the white teachers": Baldwin, "Dark Days," p. 661.

13 "Education is on the increase": Jessie Carney Smith, ed., *Notable Black American Women* (Detroit: Gale, 1992), p. 30. In 1928, Gastrude married a second time, to Dr. Vernon C. Ayer, district health officer in Harlem. He died on April 22, 1976. *New York Age* spelled her name as both Ayers and Ayer in a February 2, 1935, article announcing her appointment as principal.

14 She was eighty: Smith, ed., *Notable Black American Women*, p. 31. Ayer's beauty was widely known and was immortalized by German-American artist Winold Reiss in a portrait that appeared in the March 1925 edition of *Survey Graphic*, a special issue devoted to Harlem that would provide the featured articles for Alain Locke's *The New Negro*. Ayer, under the name of Elise Johnson McDougald, also wrote an article for that issue: "The Double Task: The Struggle of Negro Women for Sex and Race Emancipation."

14 "In New York City": McDougald, "The Double Task," pp. 690–91.

14 "I loved and feared": David Leeming, *James Baldwin: A Biography* (New York: Knopf, 1994), p. 13.

14 "I never really managed": Leeming, *James Baldwin*, p. 14. Baldwin biographer W. J. Weatherby erroneously lists "Bill" as Orrin Miller.

15 Along with the prospect: Wendy Smith, "Macbeth in Harlem," in *The Harlem Reader*, p. 117. Harlem may have been in upheaval by the time discussions were under way to stage the play with John Houseman as the head of the Federal Theater Project's Negro Unit in New York City. As Smith observed, "Rehearsals began with a good deal of tension in the air.

The Harlem community was not at all sure what it thought of 'Shakespeare in blackface' directed by a white man. Some African-Americans feared the production would make their race look ridiculous. One local zealot, convinced that *Macbeth*'s director was deliberately creating a travesty to humiliate blacks, attacked Welles with a razor in the Lafayette Theater lobby, apparently without hurting him" (p. 120).

16 "When Hammond died": Smith, "Macbeth in Harlem," p. 123.

16 Miller had achieved: W. J. Weatherby, *James Baldwin: Artist on Fire* (New York: Dell, 1989), p. 22.

16 "The play ran": Mona Z. Smith, *Becoming Something: The Story of Canada Lee* (New York: Faber & Faber, 2004), pp. 58–59. Later, in the spring of 1938, Canada Lee would return for an engagement at the Lafayette in *Haiti* by William Du Bois (the journalist, and not be confused with the other more famous Du Bois). In this play, the hero was Christophe, one of the leaders of the Haitian revolution who defeated the French, and each time a French soldier was killed by one of the rebels the Harlem audience went hysterical with glee.

16 In his book: Harold Cruse, *The Crisis of the Negro Intellectual,* (New York: Quill, 1944), p. 521. The interview appeared in the *New York Herald Tribune,* April 19, 1964, magazine section, p. 22. See *The Black New Yorkers,* created by the Schomburg Center for Research in Black Culture (New York: Wiley, 1999), for additional information on Anita Bush and the Lafayette Theater.

17 "I would walk": Adam Clayton Powell, Jr., *Adam by Adam: The Autobiography of Adam Clayton Powell, Jr.* (New York: Carol, 1994), p. 61. On the same page Powell indicates that the riot took place in 1937, a glaring error that throws a number of other facts into question.

18 "My family lived": Baldwin, "Dark Days," p. 658.

18   "The incident at the store": Herbert Shapiro, *White Violence and Black Response: From Reconstruction to Montgomery* (Amherst: University of Massachusetts Press, 1988), p. 262.

19   James Thompson: *New York Times*, March 21, 1935, p. 1.

19   The mayor quickly named: Ibid., pp. 1, 17. Sources disagree on whether one person or three were killed. Shapiro writes that two were killed; the *Times* listed the death of James Thompson two days after the riot; and *The Black New Yorkers* states that three were killed, with more than a hundred blacks arrested, thirty injured, and property damage estimated at $2 million.

19   One activist: Ibid., p. 17.

20   There was also a demand: Shapiro, *White Violence and Black Response*, p. 262. In 2005, the New York Commission on Human Rights, under the leadership of Patricia Gatling, released a CD-ROM version of the report from its archives.

20   "There has been some effort": James Baldwin, "Harlem–Then and Now," in Fern Marja Eckman, *The Furious Passage of James Baldwin* (New York: M. Evans & Co., 1966), pp. 53–55. The essay was researched and written in the fall of 1937 as Baldwin, then in the 9A, entered his final year at Frederick Douglass Junior High School. He and Randy Douglas were associate editors of the *Pilot*, the school's magazine.

20   "Porter took me downtown": Baldwin, "Dark Days," p. 662.

21   "I'm sure": Eckman, *The Furious Passage*, p. 52.

Chapter 2: ENCOUNTERING COUNTEE CULLEN

23   "artificial and overreaching": David Levering Lewis, introduction to *The Portable Harlem Renaissance Reader* (New York: Penguin, 1994), p. xl. With the description "artificial and overreaching," Lewis was perhaps referring to a notion posited by him and others that "the twenty-six novels, ten volumes of poetry, five Broadway plays, innumerable essays and short stories, two or three performed ballets and concerti,

and the large output of canvas and sculpture" were hardly enough to constitute a "renaissance." See David Levering Lewis, *When Harlem Was in Vogue* (New York: Oxford University Press, 1979), p. 121.

24 his college transcript: Gerald Early, ed., *My Soul's High Song: The Collected Writings of Countee Cullen, Voice of Harlem* (New York: Doubleday, 1991), p. 7. According to Early, "Cullen was to continue to state publicly that New York City was his place of birth for the rest of his life, as did his 1934 and 1938 passports, his 1928 French Identity Card, and James Weldon Johnson's headnote about Cullen in the 1931 edition of his anthology *The Book of American Negro Poetry.*"

24 A native of Maryland: Ibid., p. 12. There seems to be some discrepancy about the "Episcopal" designation in the church's title because by 1936, when Sugar Ray Robinson was learning to box in the church's basement, then called the Crescent Club, it was known as the Salem Methodist Church. See Herb Boyd with Ray Robinson II, *Pound for Pound: A Biography of Sugar Ray Robinson* (New York: Amistad, 2005), p. 24. A more extensive discussion of this issue can be found in Gilbert Osofsky's *Harlem: The Making of a Ghetto.* "Salem Memorial Mission," he writes, "was founded in a small room in Harlem in 1902 . . . the first service was attended by three women and the Reverend Cullen received nineteen cents for his efforts. Ten years later Salem Memorial Methodist Episcopal Church moved into quarters vacated by a white congregation and, in 1923, it moved again," p. 114.

25 He received his certificate: Ibid., p. 66.

25 Sources also differ: Leeming, *James Baldwin*, p. 22; Campbell, *Talking at the Gates: The Life of James Baldwin* (Berkeley: University of California Press, 1991), p. 20; Eckman, *The Furious Passage*, p. 49.

26 "a little bit colored": Kenneth B. Clark, *Dark Ghetto: Dilemmas of Social Power* (New York: Harper & Row, 1965), p. 39.

27 "Asking Mr. Cullen": *The Magpie,* Winter 1942, vol. 26, no. 1, p. 19, Baldwin papers, Schomburg Center for Research in Black Culture. The complete interview can also be found in Cullen's collected works, edited by Gerald Early.

27 interview with Julius Lester: Fred L. Standley and Louis H. Pratt, eds., "Reflections of a Maverick," in *Conversations with James Baldwin* (Jackson: University of Mississippi Press, 1989), p. 223. The interview originally appeared in the *New York Times Book Review,* May 27, 1984.

28 "You see": Ibid., p. 223.

28 "Its row of brick": Roi Ottley, *New World A-Coming: Inside Black America* (New York: Houghton Mifflin, 1943), p. 180.

29 Done in black face: Bruce Kellner, ed., *The Harlem Renaissance: A Historical Dictionary for the Era* (New York: Methuen, 1984), p. 344.

30 "Well, I'm very good": Eckman, *The Furious Passage,* p. 60.

30 "There was a less tangible": Leeming, *James Baldwin,* p. 22.

31 Cullen may have: Ted Gottfried, *James Baldwin: Voice from Harlem* (New York: Franklin Watts, 1997), p. 24.

32 "At that time": Ibid., p. 24.

Chapter 3: LANGSTON HUGHES

34 Depending on who: Julius Lester, 1984, *New York Times Book Review,* p. 223; Quincy Troupe, 1989.

34 "He has zoomed": Charles H. Nichols, ed., *Arna Bontemps–Langston Hughes Letters, 1925–1967* (New York: Dodd, Mead and Company, 1980), Feb. 17, 1948.

35 "I just didn't know": Arnold Rampersad, *The Life of Langston Hughes,* vol. II (New York: Oxford University Press, 2002), p. 160.

36 "low-down story": Ibid., p. 205; Nichols, *Letters,* Feb. 8, 18, 1953.

36 "That Baldwin's viewpoints": Rampersad, *The Life of Langston Hughes*, p. 296.

37 "an unfortunate and unbridgeable gap": Ibid., p. 207.

39 "All of Harlem": Baldwin, *Notes of a Native Son* (Boston: Beacon Press, 1957), p. 57.

39 "congested with people": Rampersad, p. 297.

39 "The projects in Harlem": Baldwin, *Nobody Knows My Name* (New York: Dell, 1961), p. 60.

39 "The small town": Lofton Mitchell, in *Freedomways* (Fall 1964), p. 469.

40 he recalled this meeting: *Letters*, July 9, 1958.

40 "It is a curiously juvenile book": Rampersad, p. 335.

41 "we smiled a bit": Hedgeman, *The Trumpet Sounds*, p. 173.

42 Ross Posnock agrees: Ross Posnock, *Color & Culture: Black Writers and the Making of the Modern Intellectual* (Cambridge, Mass.: Harvard University Press, 2000), p. 224.

42 "After we ordered": Leeming, *James Baldwin*, p. 159.

43 "It is owned": Clarke, introduction to *Harlem, U.S.A.*

44 "I remember very well": Aimé Césaire, *Discourse on Colonialism* (New York: Monthly Review Press, 2000), p. 87.

44 "Césaire is a caramel-colored man": Baldwin, "Princes and Powers," in *Nobody Knows My Name*, p. 38.

Chapter 4: SANCTUARY

47 "I use the word 'religious'": Baldwin, *The Fire Next Time* (New York: Dell, 1962), p. 27.

48 "We're tired": Schomburg Center, *Black New Yorkers*, p. 240. This was uttered by Reverend Lorenzo King of St. Mark's Protestant Episcopal Church.

49 "It would be impossible": *New York Times*, January 1, 1939.

49 "I graduated from Douglass": Eckman, *The Furious Passage*, p. 62.

50 "My own attitude": Baldwin made this comment during a roundtable discussion with Nathan Glazer, Gunnar Myrdal, and Sidney Hook. Norman Podhoretz was the moderator and the topic was "Liberalism and the Negro." A transcript of this discussion can be found in the digital archives (www.commen tarymagazine.com) of *Commentary* magazine, March 1964.

51 "Long before": Eckman, *The Furious Passage*, p. 82.

52 "Elder Sobers": Interview with George Baldwin, June 25, 2006. In *Go Tell It on the Mountain*, the church was called the Temple of the Fire Baptized.

52 "I didn't believe": Eckman, *The Furious Passage*, p. 83.

53 "Shortly after I turned sixteen": Baldwin, "Here Be Dragons," in *The Price of the Ticket*, p. 681.

54 "gave me my first drink": Baldwin, *Tell Me How Long the Train's Been Gone* (New York: Vintage, 1998), p. 244.

Chapter 5: DEATH IN HARLEM

57 "blind smoldering resentment": Haygood, *King of the Cats* (New York: Houghton-Mifflin, 1993), p. 97.

57 "Blind, unreasoning fury": *The Evidence of Things Not Seen* (New York: Holt, Rinehart, and Winston, 1985), p. 33.

58 "The riot had profound": Kenneth Robert Janken, *White: The Biography of Walter White, Mr. NAACP* (New York: The New Press, 2001), p. 277.

58 "I left in Harlem": James Baldwin file, Schomburg Center for Research in Black Culture, Feb. 14, 1943.

59 "There is a sense": Margaret Mead and James Baldwin, *A Rap on Race* (Philadelphia: J. P. Lippincott, 1973), p. 41.

60 "When James did go home": Gottfried, *James Baldwin*, p. 33.

60 "James helped": Interview with George Baldwin, Oct. 1, 2006.

61 "Though he split": Interview with Quincy Troupe.

61 "In my opinion": Martha Biondi, *To Stand and Fight: The*

Struggle for Civil Rights in Postwar New York City (Cambridge, Mass: Harvard University Press, 2003), p. 27.

62 "The horrendous dishonesty": Leeming, *James Baldwin*, p. 54.

62 "When Jimmy decided": Interview with George Baldwin, Oct. 1, 2006.

Chapter 6: MALCOLM X

65 "I first met Malcolm Little": Interview with Clarence Atkins.

66 "when he compared their lives": Weatherby, *James Baldwin*, p. 299.

66 got along reasonably well: Leeming, *James Baldwin*, p. 188.

67 I saw Malcolm: Baldwin, *The Price of the Ticket*, p. 497.

68 "I sometimes found myself": Baldwin, *The Fire Next Time* (New York: Dell, 1964), p. 68.

68 "It is quite impossible": Baldwin, *The Price of the Ticket*, p. 265.

69 "When Malcolm X": Baldwin, *The Price of the Ticket*, p. 357.

69 "When James Baldwin came in": James H. Cone, *Martin & Malcolm & America: A Dream or a Nightmare?* (New York: Orbis Books, 2005), p.117.

70 "The speech still had fire": John Lewis, *Walking with the Wind* (New York: Harcourt Brace, 1998), p. 230.

71 "What Malcolm tells them": Clark, *Conversations with James Baldwin*, p. 43.

71 "pseudo-revolt": *Egyptian Gazette*, August 17, 1964.

72 "When Baldwin took": Interview with Louis Lomax, 1963, TeachingAmericanHistory.org.

72 Malcolm would have been: *New York Times*, May 25, 1963.

73 "weapons for years": *New York Times*, July 27, 1964.

73 "They don't know anything": Victor Lasky, *Robert F. Kennedy, The Myth and the Man* (New York: Trident, 1968), p. 188.

73 "You don't know what the hell": Lester and Irene David,

Bobby Kennedy: The Making of a Folk Hero (New York: Dodd, Mead and Company, 1986), p. 190.

74 in fact was a third-generation: John Henry Cutler, *Ed Brooke: Biography of a Senator* (New York: Bobbs Merrill, 1972), p. 298.

74 "After Baldwin": Evan Thomas, *Robert Kennedy: His Life* (New York: Simon & Schuster, 2000), p. 245.

74 In 1963: Kenneth O'Reilly and David Gallen, *Black Americans: The FBI Files* (New York: Carroll & Graf, 1994), p. 69.

75 *Well, Niggers don't own*: From "Stagerlee Wonders," in James Baldwin, *Jimmy's Blues: Selected Poems* (New York: St. Martin's Press, 1985), p.16.

76 "I do believe": Clark, *Conversations with James Baldwin*, p. 100.

76 "Malcolm, finally": Baldwin, *The Price of the Ticket*, p. 499.

77 "It isn't only the landlord": John O. Killens and Fred Halstead, eds., *Harlem Stirs* (New York: Marzani & Munsell, 1964).

77 "Well, my reaction": *New York Post*, May 1, 1964.

78 And some believed: See William W. Sales Jr.'s *From Civil Rights to Black Liberation* (Boston: South End Press, 1994), p. 157.

78 "This is the first time": Cone, p. 305.

78 Nothing could have been: Baldwin, *The Price of the Ticket*, p. 498.

79 "'Are you trying to tell me'": Clark, *Conversations with James Baldwin*, p. 259.

79 "What made him unfamiliar": Baldwin, *The Price of the Ticket*, p. 499.

80 "The British press": Weatherby, *James Baldwin*, p. 301.

80 "color is not important": *New York Times*, June 21, 1963.

81 "As a writer": Baldwin files, Tamiment Library, New York University.

83 "To make a long story short": Clark, *Conversations with James Baldwin*, p. 167.

84 he "didn't know how to handle Elijah": Ralph Wiley, *What*

Black People Should Do Now: Dispatches from Near the Vanguard (New York: Ballantine Books, 1993), p. 191.

Chapter 7: THE HARLEM SIX

87   the Martinsville Seven: The *Daily Worker* described the case in 1949: "On January 8, 1949, a group of seven young men sexually assaulted a thirty-two-year-old woman in the city of Martinsville, Virginia. When the details of the offense were reported in the local newspaper, residents of the town were shocked that such a thing could happen in their community. The crime angered a lot of people. The suspects had been drinking all that day and later testimony indicated that at least four of the men were intoxicated during the event. The victim, who was married to a local store manager, suffered severe physical and psychological injuries. She was hospitalized and kept in seclusion until court proceedings began during April of 1949. All seven attackers were black. The victim was white. Despite the inflammatory racial aspects of the case, the judicial atmosphere was calm and deliberate. Too deliberate, some said, 'The defense attorneys stood idly by while the prosecution, the judge and the all-white jury, with unbelievable speed-up, railroaded the seven,' said one newspaper account of the trials" (*Daily Worker*, June 1, 1949).

88   They came "into the room": Baldwin, *The Price of the Ticket*, p. 415.

89   "No one had": Sergeant Issac Woodard experienced a similar tragedy on February 26, 1946, when he was returning home after serving a stint in the army. Woodard, accused of making too much noise by a bus driver, was snatched from the bus near Aiken, South Carolina. He was among several soldiers from Camp Gordon, black and white, who were celebrating their new status as civilians. When the driver asked one of the white soldiers to come to the front of the bus—in keeping with

the state's segregation laws—the soldier refused. When Woodard requested a stop so he could relieve himself, the driver refused and an argument ensued between them. At the next town the driver called the sheriff and reported the incident. The sheriff forcibly removed Woodard from the bus, but, according to the sheriff, Woodard resisted arrest and tried to take the blackjack the sheriff was using to subdue him. During the trial, one of the first civil rights cases heard in the state, Woodard offered his version of what happened. However, the all-white jury believed the sheriff, not the blinded Woodard, who had been beaten and then had his eyes gouged out by the sheriff's billy club. The incident aroused the nation and hundreds sent letters to President Truman asking him to intercede to mete out justice. Truman acted and out of this came the National Emergency Committee Against Violence. Truman would later appoint a blue-ribbon commission and issue Executive Order 9808, an edict demanding freedom from fear.

89 "Within hours": Conrad Lynn, *There Is a Fountain* (Westport, Conn.: Lawrence Hill, 1979).

90 "My report": Baldwin, *The Price of the Ticket*, p. 418.

91 Arthur Barron: *New York Times*, May 11, 1984.

92 "In Lagos": *The Autobiography of Malcolm X* (New York: Ballantine, 1973), p. 402.

92 "The press": Ibid, p. 418.

93 "African liberation": *The Black Bolshevik*.

94 "I picked the cotton": *New York Times*, February 19, 1965.

94 "I don't want you to worry": Letter, July 26, 1966, Baldwin files, Schomburg Center.

95 Funds were also being raised: *New York Times*, August 25, 1967.

95 "The case that was presented": Lynn, *There Is a Fountain*, p. 12.

96 "No one in Harlem": Baldwin, *The Price of the Ticket*, p. 424.

96 "But we were on top of the case": Interview with Elombe Brath, September 6, 2006.

97 He was later released: Truman Nelson, *The Torture of Mothers* (Boston: Beacon Press, 1968), p. 92.

97 "I don't believe any gun": *New York Times*, August 22, 1971.

98 "He said there was evidence": Lynn, *There Is a Fountain*, p. 33.

99 "A crime": Baldwin, *The Price of the Ticket*, p. 422.

99 "They came away": Lynn, *There Is a Fountain*, p. 33.

100 "Now, what I have said": Baldwin, *The Price of the Ticket*, p. 420.

Chapter 8: THE JEWISH QUESTION

104 "Jews in Harlem": Baldwin, *Notes of a Native Son*, p. 48.

105 "Baldwin and I": Sol Stein, *James Baldwin and Sol Stein: Native Sons* (New York: One World/Ballantine Books, 2005), p. 6.

106 "It often annoyed him": Weatherby, *James Baldwin*, p. 29.

107 "For nothing is fixed": Baldwin, *Nothing Personal*.

107 "My best friend": Baldwin, *The Fire Next Time*, p. 54.

108 "He had a curious": Eckman, *The Furious Passage*, p. 81.

108 "In 1946": Biondi, *To Stand and Fight*, p. 13.

109 "jim crowism": Horne, *Black Liberation/Red Scare–Ben Davis and the Communist Party* (Newark: University of Delaware Press, 1994), p. 90.

111 "They were forced to quit": *New York Times*, February 28, 1967.

112 "We hated them": Baldwin, *The Price of the Ticket*, p. 425.

112 "it is immoral": Esther Cooper Jackson, ed., *Freedomways Reader* (Boulder, Colo.: Westview Press, 2000), p. 209.

112 "Jewish liberalism": Cruse, *The Crisis of the Negro Intellectual*, p. 405. In *Soul Power* (Durham, N.C.: Duke University Press, 2006), Cynthia Young notes the extent to which Cruse was so passionately concerned about making–and winning–a point that he was often unable to see the complexity of the race question.

Young, discussing how Cruse repudiated Ossie Davis and Ruby Dee merely because of their association with whites, argues, "Narrowly focusing on whether or not white people participated in a given cultural institution blinded Cruse to the fact that race might be one–but not the only or the most important–criteria for establishing a shared cultural and political identity" (p. 84).

113 "In any event": Cruse, *The Crisis of the Negro Intellectual*, pp. 413–14.

113 "It is possible": Baldwin, "Sweet Lorraine," *The Price of the Ticket*, p. 446.

114 "like my baby sister": Clark, *Conversations with James Baldwin*, p. 156.

114 "The first white man": "An Open Letter to the Born Again," *The Price of the Ticket*, p. 655.

115 "He never knew": Baldwin, *No Name in the Street*, p. 476.

115 Like the fighters: In David Remnick's biography of Muhammad Ali, *King of the World*, there is a long description of this meeting. It's rewarding to hear Baldwin's estimation of the fighters and his typical ambivalence, recognizing both fighters as products of a poor, black experience in America. W. J. Weatherby talked about the "unsettled differences" between Baldwin and Mailer, and the "chill" between them at the fight. See Weatherby, *James Baldwin*, p. 223.

116 Osby Mitchell: Quincy Troupe, ed., *James Baldwin: The Legacy* (New York: Simon & Schuster, 1989), p. 206.

116 Baldwin at the College of Staten Island: Interview with Quincy Troupe, October 1, 2006.

117 "innocent and provincial": William Jelani Cobb, ed., *The Essential Harold Cruse: A Reader* (New York: Palgrave, 2002), p. 77.

118 "We all hated Rabinowitz": Baldwin, *Tell Me How Long the Train's Been Gone*, p. 16.

118 "You want me to peddle my ass": Baldwin, *Just Above My Head* (New York: Dell, 1978), pp. 409–10.

120 denying the allegation and supporting Baldwin: Leeming,
     James Baldwin, p. 365.

122 The spokesman for Frost: *New York Times,* June, 10, 1971.

123 A portion of their exchange: Mead and Baldwin, *A Rap on
     Race,* pp. 214–15.

Chapter 9: HARLEM, REAL AND IMAGINED

128 "outing": Douglas Field, in contrast, supports several biogra-
     phers' suggestion of an undertone of "sexualized spirituality"
     in Baldwin's writings prior to *Giovanni's Room:* "As Baldwin
     said in an interview with the *Village Voice* in 1985, 'terror of
     the flesh . . . is a doctrine which has led to untold horrors.'
     Throughout *Go Tell It on the Mountain,* he emphasizes the
     physicality of worship and the thin line between religious and
     sexual exertion. As the storefront congregation worships, 'their
     bodies gave off an acrid, steamy smell' which is not far off the
     'the unconquerable odour . . . of dust, and sweat' surrounding
     the 'sinners' in the street outside. During worship, as Baldwin
     repeatedly reminds us, the physical body can be hidden but
     not forgotten behind the holy robes: Elisha's 'thighs moved
     terribly against the cloth of his suit.'" Douglas Field, "Reread-
     ings," *Guardian,* November 15, 2003.

129 "If ever, indeed": Baldwin, *Notes of a Native Son,* p. 112.

129 "the bright prose": Campbell, *Talking at the Gates,* p. 104.

131 "And he'd always been": Baldwin, "Sonny's Blues" in *Going to
     Meet the Man* (New York: Vintage Books, 1995), p. 103.

131 "Some escaped the trap": Ibid, p. 112.

132 A ghetto, he concluded: Baldwin, *The Price of the Ticket,* p. 210.

132 "Baldwin, inexcusably": Mayfield, "And Then Came Baldwin,"
     p. 167.

133 "The inhabitants of Riverton": Baldwin, "Fifth Avenue,
     Uptown," in *The Price of the Ticket,* pp. 209–10.

134 "The beat—in Harlem": Baldwin, *Another Country* (New York: Vintage, 1993), p. 7.

136 "No, I'm not": Baldwin, *Blues for Mr. Charlie* (New York: Dell, 1964), p. 36.

140 "at the mercy of whites": *New York Times*, May 19, 1974.

142 When Webster suspects: Baldwin, "The Gospel Singer," in *Just Above My Head* (New York: Dell, 1978), p. 212.

142 "We came into the sunlight": Baldwin, *Just Above My Head*, p. 282.

144 "he never really accounts for": Albert Murray, *The Omni-Americans* (New York: Avon, 1970), pp. 214–15.

144 "The beautiful children": Baldwin, *Another Country*, p. 114.

147 "On the top floor": *Essence*, November 1996, p. 112.

Chapter 10: CRUSE'S CRISIS

149 "The Harlem Ghetto": Cruse, *The Essential Harold Cruse*, p. 82.

151 "I have in mind": "Liberalism, Pluralism and the American Family Fantasy," *Commentary*, March 1964, p. 42.

152 "As a boy": Harold Cruse, *Rebellion or Revolution?* (New York: William Morrow, 1968), p. 11.

152 "I spent the years": Ibid., pp. 12–13.

153 "I came through it": Ibid.

155 "by the pundits": Cruse, *The Essential Harold Cruse*, p. 29.

155 "It's like Sidney Poitier": Fred L. Standley and Louis H. Pratt, eds., *Conversations with James Baldwin* (Jackson: University Press of Mississippi, 1989), p. 33.

155 "I don't consider myself": Jordan Elgrably and George Plimpton, "The Art of Fiction LXXVIII: James Baldwin:" in *Conversations with James Baldwin*, pp. 240–41, and *Paris Review*, vol. 26 (Spring 1984), pp. 49–82. During an interview with Ida Lewis of *Essence* magazine, while she was visiting Paris

in 1970, Baldwin stressed this point. "Yes, I played two roles. I never wanted to be a spokesman, but I suppose it was something that had to happen. But that is over now." See Abraham Chapman, ed., *New Black Voices* (New York: Mentor, 1972), p. 411.

156   "Baldwin had neither": Henry Louis Gates, Jr., *Thirteen Ways of Looking at a Black Man* (New York: Random House, 1997), p. 11.

156   "consistent with his Marxist beliefs": Margaret Walker, *Richard Wright: Daemonic Genius* (New York: Amistad, 1988), p. 236.

157   "I believe my son was sent": Interview with Mamie Bradley Mobley, January 12, 2002.

158   "comments at some length": Daryl Dance, "Black American Writers: Bibliographical Essays," M. Thomas Inge, et al., *Black American Literature Forum*, p. 110. Cruse's complete footnote reads: "Here, the white liberal character, Parnel James, comes across more as a rather naively-drawn human prop for the action, than a character in depth; so sympathetically portrayed as to border on the maudlin, despite the author's professed view of white liberals." Cruse, *The Crisis of the Negro Intellectual*, p. 200.

158   "This failure": Cruse, *The Crisis of the Negro Intellectual*, p. 194.

159   "It is personally painful to me": Ibid., p. 301.

160   "nobility stemmed": Paul Robeson, Jr., "Paul Robeson: Voice of a Century," *Black Collegian*, http://www.black-collegian .com/issues/1998-02/probeson.shtml. "Robeson, lives, overwhelmingly in the hearts and minds of the people whom he touched," Baldwin wrote in the letter protesting the play, "the people for whom he was an example, the people who gained from him the power to perceive and the courage to exist. It is not a sentimental question. He lived in our times, we live

in his . . . It is a matter of bearing witness to that force which moved among us." This excerpt appears in Paul Robeson, Jr.'s book *The Undiscovered Paul Robeson: An Artist's Journey, 1898-1939* (New York: Wiley, 2001). The letter was originally printed in the *Village Voice*, March 27, 1978.

160   "in the days": Philip S. Foner, ed., *Paul Robeson Speaks* (New York: Brunner/Mazel, 1978), p. 44.

160   "I did not go through": Baldwin in the Foreword to Bobby Seale, *A Lonely Rage* (New York: Times Book, 1978), p. ix.

161   "For the first five years": Paul Robeson with Lloyd Brown, *Here I Stand* (Boston: Beacon, 1988), p. xxiv. In the book's appendix, Robeson expanded this discussion: "It is especially heartening to me to see the active and often heroic part that leading Negro artists—singers, actors, writers, comedians, musicians—are playing today in the freedom struggle. Today it is the Negro artist who does *not* speak out who is considered to be out of line, and even the white audiences have largely come around to accepting the fact that the Negro artist is—and has every right to be—quite 'controversial' " (written August 28, 1964).

162   "Would that the artist": Julian Mayfield, "And Then Came Baldwin," in J. H. Clarke, ed., *Harlem, U.S.A.* (A&B Books, 1971), p. 157.

162   "If Mayfield's words": Peniel E. Joseph, *Waiting 'Til the Midnight Hour: A Narrative History of Black Power in America*, (New York: Henry Holt, 2006), p. 70.

163   "the reverse side": Cruse, *The Crisis of the Negro Intellectual*, pp. 485–87.

163   Two years earlier: This group must have been the Association of Artists for Freedom, which sponsored a number of forums, including one on "The Black Revolution and The White Backlash" at Town Hall on June 15, 1964. Clarence Jones was the organization's counsel and Bill Tatum was the secretary.

Thanks to Susan Tatum for providing me with a verbatim report of that meeting, at which Baldwin was not present.

164   Cruse wasn't through with Clarke: Cruse, *The Crisis of the Negro Intellectual*, p. 510.

165   "long, rambling, and cantankerous": Winston James, *Holding Aloft the Banner of Ethiopia: Caribbean Radicalism in Early Twentieth-Century America* (New York: Verso, 1998), pp. 262–69.

165   "underestimated the degree": Cobb, *The Essential Harold Cruse*, p. xvii.

165   taken to task: Beverly Guy-Sheftall, "Where Are the Black Female Intellectuals?" in Harold Cruse's *The Crisis of the Negro Intellectual Reconsidered: A Retrospective*, Jerry Gafio Watts, ed. (London: Routledge, 2004), pp. 223–24; Michele Wallace, *Invisibility Blues: From Pop to Theory* (London: Verso, 1990), p. 100; Guy-Sheftall, "Reconstructing a Black Female Intellectual Tradition: Commentary on Harold Cruse's *The Crisis of the Negro Intellectual*," *Voices of the African Diaspora: The CAAS Research Review*, vol. 9, no. 1 (Winter 1994), pp. 20–21.

166   "'Integration,' he warned": Wallace, *Invisibility Blues*, p. 100.

166   "This African challenge": Jacob Carruthers, *Intellectual Warfare* (Chicago: Third World Press, 1999), p. 194.

167   "protest and reform politics": Greg Tate, *Flyboy in the Buttermilk* (New York: Simon & Schuster, 1998), p. 198.

Chapter 11: BARAKA

169   "The middle class native intellectual": Amiri Baraka, *The Autobiography of LeRoi Jones/Amiri Baraka* (New York: Freundlich, 1984), p. 202.

170   "I had no formal definition": Ibid., p. 216.

170   "Our politics": Ibid., p. 224.

171 "to shriek the shriek": LeRoi Jones, *Home* (New York: William Morrow, 1966), p. 117.

172 "Cutting throats": Ibid., p. 120.

172 We are unfair: Jones, *Home*, p. 252.

173 "I had tried": Baraka, *The Autobiography of LeRoi Jones/Amiri Baraka*, p. 279.

173 Neither Baldwin nor Baraka: Campbell, *Talking at the Gates*, pp. 167–73. One of the most rewarding things about Campbell's biography is its discussion of the FBI and its spying on Baldwin. Through the Freedom of Information Act, Campbell pored over more than a thousand pages of documents in Baldwin's files. Writers on the left were always under surveillance by the government, but Baldwin's file was among the largest. See Ward Churchill and Jim Vander Wall, *The Cointelpro Papers: Documents from the FBI's Secret Wars Against Dissent in the United States* (Boston: South End, 1990), p. 342. In a measure typical of the FBI disinformation campaign, Baldwin was sent an anonymous communication incriminating a member of the Socialist Workers Party, charging that he had stolen funds earmarked for civil rights activity. This happened in 1964 and made Baldwin more wary of the FBI's harassment of him.

174 "There were twelve of us": Jones, "Cuba Libre," in *Home*, p. 13.

175 Puerto Rican population: Félix V. Matos-Rodriguez and Pedro Juan Hernández, *Pioneros: Puerto Ricans in New York City 1896–1948* (New York: Arcadia, 2001), p. 7.

177 "He was my older brother": William J. Harris, ed., *The LeRoi Jones/Amiri Baraka Reader* (New York: Thunder's Mouth Press, 1991), p. 454.

Afterword

181 "Richard's *Native Son*": Standley and Pratt, *Conversations with James Baldwin*, p. 253.

SELECTED BIBLIOGRAPHY

Since this book has a special angle on James Baldwin's life, with no pretensions to being a comprehensive biography, I offer here a selected bibliography of only those books I have consulted repeatedly—those scattered nearby, on and around my desk—and that themselves offer helpful resource information.

Horace A. Porter's *Stealing the Fire: The Art and Protest of James Baldwin* (Middletown, Conn.: Wesleyan University Press, 1989), includes an extensive bibliography with sections on Baldwin's books, essays, dialogues, plays, scenarios, poetry, discussions, and interviews, as well as works on Baldwin (including dissertations), and other bibliographies. A brief listing of obituaries and tributes includes those encomiums delivered at Baldwin's funeral.

In *James Baldwin: A Biography* (New York: Knopf, 1994), David Leeming offers a well-organized, chronological bibliography that he compiled with the assistance of Lisa Gitelman. One can follow Baldwin as his career develops year by year, beginning with his book reviews in 1947 in such publications as the *Nation, New Leader,* and *Commentary.* This extends to 1989, two years after Baldwin's death. A nice benefit of this structure is being able to see the often revealing correlations of Baldwin's fiction and nonfiction through time.

W. J. Weatherby's *James Baldwin: Artist on Fire* (New York: Dell, 1989) has no stand-alone bibliography but does have source notes, though the list is modest. James Campbell's *Talking at the Gates: A Life of James Baldwin* (Berkeley: University of California Press, 1991), has a bibliography that is shorter than Leeming's but also weaves Baldwin's works in a neat chronology.

There is a mixture of relevant and incidental books in the bibliography of Stanley Macebuh's *James Baldwin: A Critical Study* (New York: Third Press, 1973), which is to some degree determined by the author's theme. More sources are found at the end of each chapter. Since the book was published in 1973, many later works are absent.

Ted Gottfried's *James Baldwin* (New York: Franklin Watts, 1997), has a young adult appeal, which by no means reduces its usefulness. Like the book itself, the bibliography is short. The suggested readings are helpful.

James Baldwin: A Collection of Critical Essays (Englewood Cliffs, N.J.: Prentice-Hall, 1974) edited by Keneth Kinnamon, has a chronology listing some of the important dates in Baldwin's life. For a more detailed timeline see *James Baldwin: The Collected Essays,* edited by Toni Morrison (New York: Library of America, 1998).

Because Fern Marja Eckman's *The Furious Passage of James Baldwin* (New York: M. Evans, 1966) was developed from a series of interviews, there is a unique combination of bibliography and notes.

In terms of focus and length, *James Baldwin: The Legacy*

(New York: Simon & Schuster, 1989), edited by Quincy Troupe, is just about right, with books by Baldwin, about him, and interviews. The inclusion of the forewords and introductions that Baldwin wrote is valuable.

Indispensable to this project was Sol Stein's *Native Sons* (New York: One World/Ballantine, 2005). Among its most rewarding elements are newly discovered correspondence and photographs, all of which give Baldwin's great humanity added depth. It has a rich account of Baldwin's early years as viewed by a friend from another culture.

Conversations with James Baldwin (Jackson: University Press of Mississippi, 1989), edited by Fred L. Standley and Louis H. Pratt, is a trove of information. There are few better authorities on the life of Baldwin than Standley and Pratt.

Daryl Dance's bibliographic essay on Baldwin in *Black American Writers* (New York: St. Martin's, 1978) is a lode-stone of brief but penetrating analysis. (It is reminiscent of what John Hope Franklin offers at the end of *From Slavery to Freedom*). *James Baldwin: The Price of the Ticket*, a 1990 documentary directed by Karen Thorsen, is not only visually stunning, but gives Baldwin the extra dimension that only a camera can.

Much of the material acquired from numerous magazines, periodicals, and newspapers is listed in the notes. Today's researcher is ably abetted by the Internet, and it is such a joy to discover that many of the long-standing publications—and a few that no longer exist—have been digitized and archived on websites. Being able to access articles on Baldwin via the Internet saved me money, time, and energy tracking down obscure sources, though, of course, one has to be ever vigilant and mindful of the Net's flaws and of unreliable resources.

CREDITS AND PERMISSIONS

Index